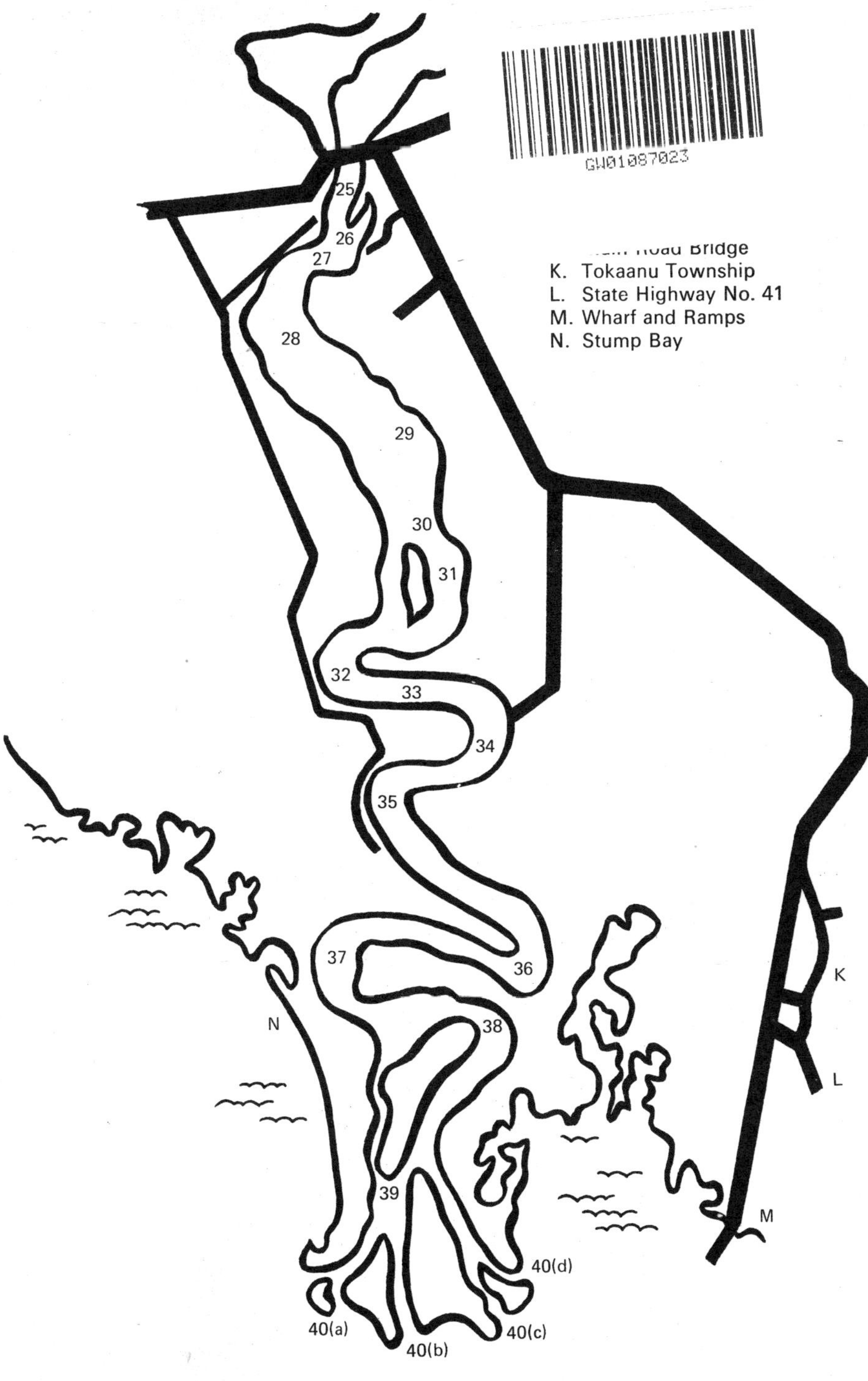
K. Tokaanu Township
L. State Highway No. 41
M. Wharf and Ramps
N. Stump Bay
25
26
27
28
29
30
31
32
33
34
35
36
37
38
39
40(a)
40(b)
40(c)
40(d)
N
K
L
M

Trout of the Tongariro

Wishing you a very happy birthday.

Love

Jonathan

1976

TROUT of the TONGARIRO

Tony Jensen

A.H.& A.W. REED
Wellington Sydney London

First published 1974

A. H. & A. W. REED LTD
182 Wakefield Street, Wellington
51 Whiting Street, Artarmon, NSW 2064
11 Southampton Row, London WC1B 5HA
also
29 Dacre Street, Auckland
165 Cashel Street, Christchurch

ISBN O 589 00858 7

Library of Congress Catalogue Card Number: 73-94057

Typeset by Express Typesetting Service Ltd, Christchurch
Printed by Dai Nippon Printing Co. (Hong Kong) Ltd

DEDICATION

For my mother,
Winifred Jensen of Napier,
and for my wife, Josephine

CONTENTS

LIST OF ILLUSTRATIONS

ACKNOWLEDGMENTS

AN AUTHOR ENTERS A page entitled "Acknowledgments" with a feeling of fear deep-seated in the stomach.

The book is completed, the last i dotted and the last t crossed, apart from, one suspects, the final, doubt-ridden, slow resigned reading which seems to confirm every innermost trepidation which has haunted him from the time he first picked up his pencil.

What if now he omits to mention someone who has been of inestimable value to him during the time the book is being compiled?

In the fervent hope that I have forgotten no one, and placing them in alphabetical order so that each and every one will know that equal importance is attached to their contributions I thank:

Susan Anderson, my artist.

Rex Forrester,
National Publicity Studios } for photographs
Shirley Parkinson

The Wildlife Division of the Internal Affairs Department for permission to use their updated Condition Factor Chart.

Kevin Murphy, Tongariro Hatchery Manager and Trevor Thompson, Chief Field Officer who, between them, know more of things piscatorial than the trout themselves. And overseas and local anglers who have contributed so much knowledge and not a few anecdotes.

TONY JENSEN

FOREWORD

To be asked to write the foreword to Tony Jensen's book on the Taupo basin trout-fishing is indeed a compliment. I have fished these waters consistently since I returned to New Zealand in 1948 but I find there is still much to learn—and a book like this cuts one down to size.

Though I have read books on trout-fishing from Isaak Walton through G. E. M. Skues, Henry Williamson and R. Haig-Brown to Admiral Hickling's classic *Freshwater Admiral* I have never read a more interesting, amusing nor readable coverage of the local scene.

Knowing Tony for many years, and fishing with him often, one soon learns what a thoughtful, observant, experienced though humble fisherman he is. He writes as he speaks—with ease. The poignant drama of the elusive giant "brown" in the Blind Mouth Reach is, to me, the highlight of the book. On the other hand one comes across excerpts that make one burst out laughing.

Tony "guided" for an overseas friend of mine whose verdict was—"Wonderful expertise, Wonderful fishing, Wonderful company!"

Here is a book that must be a success, for it holds one's intense interest throughout.

TURANGI
1974

R. L. KENNEDY

PREFACE

ANY ENDEAVOUR TO write about the skills, joys and frustrations of angling for trout must, of necessity, leave much unsaid. In advance then, to those of you who know and love our river, I say forgive the omissions, bear with the obvious and try, as we work our way through a couple of your favourite pools, to relive those moments of happiness you have experienced in them.

The veteran angler of these wonderful waters may have nothing to learn from these pages, and for this I offer no apology. He has had his triumphs, known the day when a complete tyro has outfished him and, if time has been kind to him, is already planning his next trip. Show me, though, a man who takes his fishing earnestly and is no longer prepared to seek a different method or try a new technique, and I shall describe a man with a closed mind to any new adventure.

Basically then, this book attempts to assist a new chum to a new sport, and to help him to receive his fair share of the waters' bounty coupled with a generous portion of delight at the beauty which is the Tongariro River.

I was nine when I was given my first fly rod and, upon reflection, I wonder that I ever fished beyond the age of ten. Nine feet of telescopic steel weighing, from a small boy's infallible memory, about 20 ounces, it was whippy enough to have been indestructible if set upright and hit by an express train. The level silk line which accompanied this proudly wielded possession had seen better days; perforated and infuriatingly sticky, it looked and cast like knitting wool impregnated with molasses. These were, nevertheless, Depression years and lucky indeed was a lad with any tackle worthy of the name. Undaunted, some weeks and innumerable flies later, during which time I can recall actually crying with frustration at that unmentionable line, I hooked and landed my first trout. I was fishing the Waikaretaheke—the outlet stream of Lake Waikaremoana—without much hope, totally without skill and, by this time, almost without enjoyment when the miracle happened. It must have been through Divine intervention, because to the best of my knowledge no fish has ever been taken by such a poor, sloppy, short, badly presented cast either before or since.

That incredible line had become hopelessly entangled in the coils in my left hand, perhaps even glued to itself or my fingers, and the Royal Coachman was lying, dying, in a backwater where no self-respecting trout would condescend to lie unless it were on a self-imposed starvation diet. Sighing, close to tears, I once again peeled the tacky mess from my digits, dropped it in the water and lifted the tip of that weightlifter's rod for another cast.

It stayed down. The line moved slowly toward the opposite bank. Uncomprehending I watched, and still it moved. Something, dear God, was alive on the other end.

I did not strike in the accepted sense of the word. I did not raise the tip of the rod. Every instruction drilled into me by my grandfather, W. K. (Bill) Carter of Gisborne and Waikaremoana and his well-meaning friends was forgotten in this moment of truth. I ran; skinny, bare, half-frozen legs, pushing, pumping at the water like pistons. Sideways like a crab to be sure, but I ran, rod pointing at the spot where the line entered the water like a cowboy's 44 carbine covering Billy the Kid. Had I been able to do as well on land as I did in those few yards to the beach, I should have been the boy wonder of that year's 1936 Olympics. Over the last few treacherous, moss-covered boulders to the safety of the grassy bank, and still I ran, towing, pulling, hauling my first trout to inevitable and ignominious doom.

Hooked inescapably through the lower jaw, and with something akin to a hawser as a gut leader attached to the fly, it had been landed in world-record time for the distance. Again relying on a youngster's memory, I swear it died from shock, too surprised at its dreadful manhandling to quiver, let alone flap, on that final shore.

And the boy? Still at the run, I unhooked that silver prize and headed the three miles for home, only slowing to a nonchalant swagger whenever someone came into view. It weighed, I recall, just 2 pounds 4 ounces, but to me it equalled, nay surpassed, anything that Ernest Hemingway in later years could conjure up for his *Old Man and The Sea.*

I had hooked my first fish and, in turn, I was hooked as an angler for the rest of my days.

That first experience, despite moderate success in the rather too many years which have followed, is unforgettable and unforgotten, and for those of you who have still to realise the thrill of your first rainbow, I can state categorically that it will live with you throughout your lifetime.

Small boys reach manhood as small boys will, and following ten years as a golf professional (it took me that long to realise I was never going to threaten the Arnold Palmers and Jack Nicklauses of the era) I found myself in Turangi at the southern end of Lake Taupo, living within a stone's throw of the Tongariro and busying myself as a professional guide to predominantly overseas anglers.

It is a life I love and one which I hope to maintain for many a year. Through it I have made many lasting friendships with people from all walks of life and all areas of the world. It is an axiom which you, dear novice, will be unable to refute, angling friends remain friends.

While writing these pages I've been confronted with a perplexing problem: New Zealand is rapidly approaching the metricated age where a 5-pound fish will weigh 2.27 kilograms and a 9-foot rod will become a 2.75 metre one. Just how long it will take the less intelligent ones of us to grasp these peculiar innovations I don't know, but it will not be overnight, and certainly it won't be happening to our American visitors for several years yet. Accordingly I've decided to stick to the old familiar measurements, but with one notable exception: the Wildlife Service of the Internal Affairs Department has been generous enough to allow me to reproduce their new Condition Factor Chart, which shows the factor in both the imperial and metric measures.

In the unlikely event of someone picking up this book in AD 2074 and failing to understand those mysterious pounds and feet he encounters on other pages—well, I shan't be here to feel sorry for him or help him out. And, moreover, a five-pounder will for ever sound like more of a fish than one reduced to two and a couple of miserable decimals!

If this book helps you to find not only an occasional rainbow or a more occasional brownie, but also comradeship on the banks of the greatest river of them all, the Tongariro, I shall be content.

TONY JENSEN

INTRODUCTION

CAN THE ATTEMPT TO write a book on the Tongariro River and its neighbouring streams spring from a spontaneous impulse?

Unlikely. Yet although it must have crossed my mind previously, it had been an idle dream, something to be stored away for old age, when time becomes less important and the hours spent fishing of necessity reduced. Something to be done—sometime . . . .

Accordingly, it is with astonishment that I find myself, pencil in hand, at this moment, preface already completed (apart from, I suspect, forty-four revisions), wondering whether I have the competence, the knowhow or the wit to make it not only informative for the beginner but, perhaps, readable for the oldtimer. Already the task seems more formidable, the challenge too one-sided, the imagined delight at its completion too many words away.

But still that nagging determination persists.

The undertaking is even more challenging, for I have read, referred to, digested and enjoyed two other authors' outstanding successes, both dealing with the same subject: at eye level, centre of shelf in the library of any fisherman worthy of the name, are the titles *Trout at Taupo* by O. S. Hintz and *Freshwater Admiral* by Harold Hickling CB, CBE, DSO, Vice Admiral RN (retd). Both these books are classics in their field. "Budge" Hintz, when not taking up cudgels in defence of the environment of the area is still imparting his trout lore to others in the pages of the *Sunday Herald* and catching a generous share of fish on his delightful Waitahanui but Admiral Hickling, alas, will battle no more rainbows from the depths of his beloved Tongariro.

The Admiral acknowledges in his preface the encouragement given to him by Mr Hintz and the latter's wish that "the task should not fall into the hands of one of the gannets". Is it small wonder that last night above my bed I heard distinctly the beating of strong wings, heard the plaintive cry and smelt the salt of the sea?

Probably there have been few decades in which change to the Tongariro has been so marked as that following the great flood of 1958 and described so vividly in *Freshwater Admiral.*

From the pleasantly sleepy hollow devoted almost exclusively to the subject of the where, when and how many of trout, a thriving bustling town of 8000 people has mushroomed. A gigantic electric power scheme brought the population, whole streets of houses sprang up seemingly overnight, shops to cater for every need blossomed in an aesthetically designed mall, strange concrete shapes appeared on hillsides, canals and tunnels snaked their way over or through hills and mountains alike. Endless streams of trucks, brimming with concrete and shingle, growl along the highway. A new and well appointed hotel caters for prodigious thirsts and offers good accommodation. Motels have appeared as if by magic, three new primary schools and a secondary school educate no fewer than 3,000 pupils and, where once only scraggy manuka grew, sealed and channelled roads crisscross each other carrying a ceaseless stream of traffic.

There are those who say "Civilisation has come to Turangi—sewerage, water supply, power, shopping and banking facilities, good roading". Then there are the others, the pre-power people who came here just to fish, to delight in a few good friends, to bask in its changelessness, to acknowledge its shortcomings of pumped water, outside toilets, limited facilities and isolated situation and to glory in them.

By 1975, we are told, the scheme will be completed and apart from a small maintenance staff and their families, the others will fold their tents and go. Turangi, the headquarters for Tongariro fishermen, will never revert to its former state, but perhaps when all the tumult and the shouting dies the Civilisationists will have left a comfortably appointed inheritance for the Isolationists.

And how does and will this affect the river, you may ask? As yet, not too drastically.

Only one major pool has been permanently sacrificed—Begg's Pool, immediately below the Waikato Falls, the most remote of the fishable waters of the Tongariro, a pool that inevitably yielded only dark fish well advanced in spawning. If a trout pool had to fall victim to the demands of electric power, it was as well that it was this one.

There have been other irritations during the progress of the undertaking which have left anglers yearning for a return of the good old days and blasphemous towards the powers-that-be who sacrificed one of the world's great fisheries to their lack of foresight in earlier years. On many occasions in the past few seasons, muddy water with the consistency of milk chocolate has suddenly surrounded fishermen's waders, a result not of torrential rain in the surrounding hills but of a miscalculation in the deposit of a few truckloads of spoil farther upstream. Possibly, because of the colossal size of the project, interruptions such as this were inevitable, but to the angling fraternity they were particularly distressing. To me they were anathema, for when, out of a clear blue sky and following a rain-free week a visitor to our shores from perhaps ten thousand miles away found himself casting into an unfishable soup, his wrath was terrifying. An Act of God one can explain, but even an Irish poet would have been hard pressed for words at times such as these.

It is in the lower river that most damage has been incurred. For three or four years the Tongariro was diverted from the lower reaches of the Swirl Pool through to the Reed while the riverbed proper was being excavated of boulders for crushing. The new man-made channel was an uninspiring, straight, uniformly deep run, uninteresting to fish and aesthetically awful, but it still held fish aplenty if one were willing to risk tackle on snags which outnumbered trout by three to one.

Meanwhile, the contractors removed the rock and the sediment flowed down river on the current, slowly filling the resting holes, and covering the shingle upon which trout choose to lie. From Reed Pool onward, many of the old established and famous pools refused to yield fish as they had done in years gone by, and it will take many floods and much scouring before they revert to their former glory.

However, so many years of research were expended before work was begun upon the scheme, so much attention devoted to conservation and erosion problems, that I do not expect any marked decline in the fishing quality of the river except in the lower reaches. On every scarred hill-face grass and trees are being planted to act as a permanent graft. If the job had to be done, it is being done as well and as kindly as possible.

The river itself will lose some volume and normal flow will be at approximately 1000 cusecs or average summer level.

As I see it, there are advantages to the relatively inexperienced in this, but some hazards as well. Wading further into the pools will make casting to the far bank a relatively easy matter for the greenhorn, the premium on long casts being reduced in some of the major pools. It is a maxim that, where not too much energy has to be expended, trout will lie for preference in the deeper, slower glide of a pool, often a difficult place in which to sink a fly rapidly enough to produce a strike. With less water as cover and a consequent slower swing of the fly through the lie, more fish could and should be taken.

The man who casts a hundred feet on the other hand—and few indeed are the pools even now where such a cast would not still be climbing as it hit the manuka on the far side (the lower stretch of Blue Pool, Cattle Rustlers', under the wires in lower Major Jones, the bottom of Bridge Lodge?)—will no doubt feel a little cheated, perhaps rightly so.

Those delightful small runs and reaches, not-too-deep but with just enough cover for a resting trout, may lack the depth to encourage a lie, and the full aggregation of angling weight may fall on the more clearly defined pools. At this stage we can only idly speculate and hope for the best.

Where man has despoiled, nature has prevailed, and the Tongariro has recovered from its fierce battering of 1958. Perhaps things aren't what they used to be, but in another decade from now I shall be telling youngsters the same thing, despite irrefutable evidence to the contrary, and what is worse, I shall be believing myself.

Great and famous pools were lost during that deluge, but new ones have formed, settled, and become providers of magnificent fishing. Torn and barren banks have had no answer to the advance of manuka, golden broom, yellow lupin and the ubiquitous fern. Kowhai bells still cascade, tempting the tui and bellbird, and fantails flirt nearby with the confidence of security. Little is left to remind one that at one short and temporary stage of its history the Tongariro was anything but beautiful.

And, most wonderful of all, the trout return year after year to their birthplace.

Tempus fugit, and ideas are developed, especially it seems with fishing tackle. Rods, once split-cane in the wealthier legions and greenheart among the neophytes or impecunious, are supplanted by lightweight and immensely powerful fibreglass. Lines of silk or terylene have been proved inferior to those of modern cellular construction designed to float, sink slowly, sink quickly or sink only at the last ten feet of their extremities. Gone are the days of endless dressing and drying. The shooting head, a development of the last few years, enables the line to be shot prodigious distances by the expert, and adequate though inconsistent spans by the mediocre caster.

Casting techniques have been markedly improved during the past few years and the adoption of the double haul by many fishermen has allowed them to fish water once far beyond their reach.

Pollution, conservation and ecology have only recently become words with which New Zealand anglers have become familiar when applied to their own environment, and it is well that so many sportsmen are now paying heed. Since 1960 the Taupo basin has not been subject to a closed season with the exception of the upper reaches of all spawning streams. On the Tongariro, fishing is permissible throughout the year from the lake proper to the entrance of the Whitikau.

In an endeavour to reduce the numbers of fish and thus provide more readily available food for others, the limit per rod per day was increased to twenty in 1962 and maintained until 1970 when it was again reduced to ten. Whether as a direct result of this action or not, the weight of rainbow improved markedly and in 1970 the average trout caught weighed 5.2 pounds. Research never rests on its laurels and as anglers we must count ourselves as the most fortunate in the world to have such dedicated men at the helm. But more of that topic later.

Greater fishing pressure on our river has brought about some ignorance of generally accepted fishing etiquette, mainly, it must be stressed, among the newcomers to the area. River hogs in greater or fewer numbers have always been with us, but somewhere in this book let the angler with even a smattering of a conscience try to identify himself. One selfish man can spoil a day's sport for a dozen others.

Ten years ago, the number of overseas anglers to visit our shores was infinitesimal. Last year more than 6000, mostly Americans, made the pilgrimage to New Zealand. Overseas river etiquette seems to be either non-existent or chaotic for the most part, but one unthinking Kiwi may convince a visitor to New Zealand that our river manners are no better than those he experiences at home.

Yes, in a decade nothing remains constant, and since Admiral Hickling wrote his book, the Tongariro and its surroundings have been subject to more change than at any other time in history. Thus, when two friends suggested I tried my hand at an updated version of a how-to and where-to fish in the area, I reluctantly agreed, and you as the reader will be the first to teach me the folly of my decision.

And so this gannet spreads its wings . . . .

CHAPTER 1

IN THE BEGINNING

CONCEIVED HIGH IN THE mountains of the Central Plateau of the North Island she gathers strength and volume as the small streams join her. Gradually she widens, gains momentum and finally, confident in the knowledge that she has surpassed all her neighbours in grandeur and spectacle, she plunges her way through the narrow entrance and thunders over the Waikato Falls. The Tongariro River is born.

Free now, she moves purposefully through the wellnigh inaccessible gorge where four miles of rapids, pools, reaches and runs fascinate the air traveller who gazes down on them. Onward still, now bordering the green pastures of the huge prison farm which bears her name, until she turns suddenly away from a sheer cliff and moves, in haste at first then more slowly, into the Fence Pool.

It is from this pool that we shall follow her throughout this book in more detail, for access to waters above the Fence is either difficult in the extreme or, because of the regulations governing access, illegal. If in our leisurely wandering down her boulder banks some of you gain a greater knowledge of the joys she has to offer, the hours spent here will not have been wasted. For the Tongariro is a complex river, often difficult of access, fierce in the extreme at times of great rainfall, and seldom suffering fools gladly. On the other hand, on a clear, bright, crackling day in autumn she is enchanting. In the upper reaches native timber stands sheer on the high banks overlooking the depths of a pool and the hidden bellbird yodels his melody over the waters. Distant upon a long horizon the craggy heights of the Kaimanawa Range, capped with an icing of snow, beckon the deerstalker, for autumn is the time of the roar and the battles of stags and the mating.

Carpets of leaves of every hue cushion your step through the winding paths which follow the river, and the air is clean and good to breathe. As the song of a few years ago has it, "On a clear day you can see for ever" and true it is at this time of the year.

It is not by accident that we have selected what our American friends call "the Fall" for the start of our expedition, for it is at the beginning of autumn that the rainbow begins the major spawning runs which continue throughout the winter and into early spring.

It is now that the hardy veteran develops a faraway look in his eye, fiddles lovingly with flyboxes, checks last season's line for signs of aging and peers anxiously for any indication of wear in his chest waders. This is the time he has been waiting for throughout the long hot summer.

The rainbows were first introduced to the Taupo fishing district in 1897 by the Wellington Acclimatisation Society. Their original homes had been the waters of the Russian and McCloud rivers of Northern California and our present-day trout have retained most of the characteristics of their steelhead ancestors.

Unable, by reason of geography, to emulate their parents' migration to the sea, they used Lake Taupo as their storehouse of food. From about the age of four to six months, up until which time they have subsisted upon natural insects in and around the rivers and streams of their birth, the trout reside in the bounty which the 238 square miles of the lake provide.

How those early trout revelled in their new conditions! Food was abundant, predators few, and the cold, deep waters of the lake suited the new arrivals to perfection. Taupo had become a home for giants and, to a lesser degree certainly, this situation still holds true. In those days long past, trout were attaining a weight of 5 lb in their first year of life and maintaining that growth for the next two years. Fish which, when landed, were found to be under 10 lb in weight were tossed contemptuously back into the water. What, after all, would others say, if one were seen to be carrying away a tiddler of that size? It would never have done for the Duke, sir. Today a 10-pounder, though not uncommon, is the pride and joy of the fortunate angler and the envy and admiration of his audience. In the past two years I have landed only four fish of this weight or more, and two of these have been brown trout. It should be pointed out, however, that a fishing guide worth his salt spends little time actually fishing during the busy months between September and May, and I know many local anglers who can boast of a tally far in excess of my four "double figures".

Personally, I am happiest when a client who has travelled perhaps 10,000 miles to sample our waters gazes in awe at a gleaming fish on the riverbank and says "Where's that camera, Tony? Unless I get a photograph of this they'll never believe me back home!"

By the early 1900s fish of 16-20 lb were far from uncommon and many of you will have seen a much-vaunted reproduction of a photograph taken in 1911 of the Hon. Percy Thelluson and friend with one day's catch taken at the mouth of the Waihaha Stream. No fewer than seventy-eight trout were taken and killed that day. None was under 12 lb in weight and no fewer than seventeen of them were 16 lb and over. To me this photograph is disturbing and faintly nauseating. It is not merely the thought of dressing so many fish at a sitting, but one wonders whether nearly half a ton of trout could be found a home in unspoiled condition in those days of no refrigeration. To be honest, my thoughts follow the line that the Hon. Percy and his fishing friend should have been made to eat every pound of their catch, preferably at one meal and without the benefits of filleting.

Forays such as this had little effect upon the ever-increasing trout population and the inevitable result was a rapidly declining weight average. The authorities came to the conclusion that there were just too many fish for the available food supply and, during the early World War I years, carried out a netting programme which resulted in no fewer than 65,000 trout being removed from the lake. How the Hon. Percy must have sighed with envy! By 1918 the trout caught were averaging under 3 lb and it appeared that the success story of the Taupo fishery had faded out for ever.

Foresight however, had paid a dividend, and with less competition for food the fish once again took a turn for the better. And what a turn! 1924 saw trout once again in the 16 lb bracket and the average had climbed to the highest in the history of the area—somewhere in excess of 10 lb.

From that date onward, with small variations during some seasons, one could look forward to an average weight per fish in the nature of something under 5 lb. That the trout have maintained this weight, or nearly so, throughout the past 40 years, must be attributed to the introduction of smelt into the lake during the middle and late 1930s. 300,000 of these, 1½-2 inches long at maturity, were liberated and, like the trout of early years, thrived and multiplied into millions. The spawning of these tiny fish takes place in lake shallows and around river mouths and, blessedly, coincides with the return of the spawned

The author in the Lower Birch Pool, Tongariro River.

trout, or kelts, from the rivers. No longer is it necessary for the weary and lean fish to forage, often vainly, for food. In packs like wolves they round up their quarry into the shallows and, mouths agape, charge the masses of smelt, churning the water white in their frenzy.

I am not convinced that the smelt constitute a highly nutritious diet for trout, but in the two and a half months of activity, this ready source of food supply enables the fish to recover from the deprivations of spawning far more rapidly than before the smelt were introduced. But more of this later; angling to smelting trout is one of the most exciting experiences a fisherman can enjoy and deserves a chapter to itself. And it shall have one.

Later still, freshwater crayfish were introduced successfully and these undoubtedly are the most favoured menu and certainly the most beneficial.

Possibly the year of 1970 supplied the best conditioned fish of the past ten years or more. Hatchery records confirm my own diary of the season when rainbows averaged 5.2 lb throughout the spawning run on the Tongariro. Better still, the condition of the trout at that time was exceptional. They were short and deep and fought with more tenacity and more endurance than I can recall in the past twenty years.

Reasons for the variations in the condition of our fish from year to year are many, and every angler I know has a theory when one particular season does not match or surpass the previous one.

Trout spawn first in their third year of life and if the season of their hatching has been uncommonly kind and free from floods, the fertilisation of ova is naturally high. Of a consequence there are thousands more fingerlings seeking food in the streams and, following the exodus to the lake, making greater demands upon the available food supply in that water. At the time of their spawning run, therefore, only a fortunate few will have found an overall sufficiency and variety of nutriment to enable them to develop into trout that an angler will be proud to display.

The opposite, of course, holds true: if, during the height of the spawning, one or more floods ravage the thinly covered redds, the loss of ova prior to hatching will be enormous, and though fish will be fewer three years later, those caught will be big and in prime condition.

The demands of the chain of hydro-electric stations along the Waikato River, the outlet of Lake Taupo, have an enormous influence upon the welfare of our fish. No longer is the lake level moderately consistent, for as water is required to keep these necessary monsters fed, the control gates at the head of the outfall are opened and it is not long before a noticeable fall in the level is evident. Should this occur during the spawning of the smelt, many of the eggs are left high and dry and perish. Once again, the trout is the one to suffer.

Predators are surprisingly few in the area. Shags are numerous and are far more successful fishermen than their human counterparts. Of these the big black is the only one not protected by law, but he is outnumbered many times over by his white-throated cousin. I do not think it is imagination which tells me that shags are becoming more plentiful on and around our waters. Personally, I detest the cowardly creatures and would gladly have them exterminated. It is alleged that they help maintain a balance of nature by concentrating on the poor and less alert fish, but I have yet to be convinced of this.

Eels, thank God, decided that the local conditions were not to their liking and, despite many attempts by the early Maoris, who valued them highly as food, to introduce them, they firmly declined to remain and disappeared from view. Many theories have been advanced for this; some claim that the pumice content of the water was too high, others that the fierce Waikato Falls prevented their return from their salty spawning grounds. I simply do not know the reason. Despite a liking for them on a plate, I am thankful that Taupo and its streams do not play host to them.

I recall one occasion when fishing the Manawatu River just south of Dannevirke which led me to prefer the eel in the pan to the one in his natural habitat. I had hooked and landed two browns and, as was the practice in these waters, had hung them on a stringer from my waist while I worked my way upstream toward the car. I had just presented a dry fly above some interesting water overhung by manuka when there was a fierce tug at my side. In the half-light of dusk my hackles rose and thoughts of taniwhas flashed through my mind. Staring down, I saw one of my precious fish bobbing up and down as if trying to pull free of its own volition.

One startled step back into shallower water revealed the most enormous eel I have ever seen in fresh water, holding on firmly to the soft underbelly of my trout. Followed a tug-of-war, with the eel at least holding its own until the belly of my fish gave up the ghost. One and three quarter trout later I climbed the bank mouthing expressive epithets concerning all eely predators and vowing never again to fish that stream with a stringer. Eels? You can keep 'em.

Poaching, of course, still has its devotees and the pitchfork, the homemade long-handled spear, the torch and one of the party posted as lookout can take quick and heavy toll of some of the smaller and more easily accessible streams. I have the feeling, however, that the practice is on the decline, thanks to the continuing vigilance of our rangers and the progressively mounting fines being meted out. When a dozen trout cost anything up to $200 the feeling among the would-be unlawful is inclining toward a couple of dollarsworth of sea fish at the local fish-and-chip shop.

The streams entering Lake Taupo are reserved for fly fishing only. Illegal fishing methods are now seldom encountered except among the very young, for no matter where one may be trying his luck, be it up at the Sand Pool or down at the Bend, the scrub is likely to part and Trevor Thomson, our Chief Ranger, to appear with the ever-polite question "Having any luck?" Somehow he always manages to spare the time to chat pleasantly until the angler has retrieved line for his next cast and an interested and expert eye seemingly casually takes in all details of the equipment being used. Especially, I might add, the terminal piece.

That poaching goes on from time to time and, I suspect, especially after dark, is not in doubt, but as a menace to the trout population it must be counted as negligible.

It was only last year, however, that the bottom of the Reed Pool produced a surprise for me. It is not often that I fish this stretch with a high-density shooting head, for the snags are numerous and solidly embedded in the heavier water. However, lunch hour was approaching and my American client had decided to take a mid-day rest before resuming his attack. It seemed a waste of time to go back to the car for another reel and, true to form, a few casts later he was held fast to a snag. Mending line downstream had no effect, nor did a manoeuvre which took us below the log. "Break it off, it's only a fly" I recommended. He leaned back, the monofilament backing gave a twang, and a new shooting head was somewhere attached to the stump. Worse still, he was using my equipment. Perhaps it was the thought of the glee on Geoff Sanderson's face as I bought my second line within a week from him, that made me decide to attempt a salvage operation. Deeper and deeper I went, the water lapping at the top of my body-waders, my bare arm groping under water for a hand-hold. I felt a twig, pulled, and it broke. Another, more solid this time, and gradually the better half of a willow tree began to emerge. Nervous assistance from my client yielded another foot and finally we dragged the dead weight to shore. Lo! my shooting head. Behold! a bonus of a full-weight forward line with ten yards of backing attached. Out of that branch we extracted, like children at a lolly-scramble, no fewer than seventeen flies and—wait for it—three spoons of assorted type.

"Thought you said this was fly-fishing water only?" said my angler. "Now I suppose you're going to tell me these were washed *up* from the lake?"

Apart, then, from natural phenomena, the ever-increasing fishing pressure, and the continuing worry of the outcome of the huge power scheme, the trout are not threatened to any marked degree.

And every autumn the first of the new season's spawners leave the lake, find their way up the quiet slower reaches of the lower river, past Dan's Creek, onward through Cherry Pool, Poplar, The Bend and Grace's Pool. There is now, they find, a little more energy required as the water increases in strength, more time needed to rest from their efforts in Down's Pool, DeLautour's Reach and the Lower Fence. Forward again through Jones Pool and into the resting lies of the Reed.

Now the river widens into a flat expanse where, before the 1958 flood, the Log, the Boat, the Nursery and the mighty Hut pools once delighted all who saw them. Here too the trout must lie, for they can feel the shallows and rapids ahead and the power of the river as it challenges the annual migration. More slowly now, they proceed through the Swirl and up the rapid into Bridge Pool, the weaker lagging behind, the stronger moving onward, ever onward, propelled by instinct to the spawning grounds of their birth.

Five miles now lie behind them and, for some, more, many more, will follow. Under the Main Highway bridge and up the heavy race to the Lonely Pool, striving mightily through the reach which bears the proud title of Judge's, they battle, their superb stamina still unimpaired after the relative quiet of the Island and the serenity of Major Jones. The journey for some will soon be over; ahead, at the tail of the Hydro Pool, these will turn up the tiny but boisterous Mangamawhitiwhiti Stream, leap its tumbling rapids and falls and move on to find a mate and reproduce.

Only a few, though, will make this diversion. The remainder swim on through the long, unrelenting flow of the Boulevard to the Kamahi, to Admiral's, around the sweep of the river to the Stag, and into the wonderful resting glide of Cattle Rustlers'. Here the tiny Hatchery Stream which enters the head of the Pool will be home for some of the migrants. Fortunate indeed are they, for after the twin Birch Pools the Tongariro becomes unrelenting in its power. Access to the Silly, the Duchess, the Shag and Red Hut is difficult in the extreme, through tumbling, white water, and the resting periods of recovery are more frequent and longer. The pure white of their bellies is changing now to a pale grey, the red on their sides becoming more pronounced, the gill-flaps darkening to crimson.

Welcome is the Poutu River entrance where it greets the Tongariro, and some will enter here for the last, long, hard slog to the spawning grounds upstream. The remainder will turn again, straining through the racing fury of the river onwards, ever onward to the Cliff, the Fan, the Blue, the Sand and the eventual haven of the Whitikau.

Overseas angler and guide in Whitikau Pool.

Countless thousands will hesitate here briefly and then, anticipating the end of their journey, will move purposefully on to the instinctively remembered birthplace.

Twelve miles of hazardous river lie behind them, and soon now a pair of weary trout will reproduce between 2000 and 3000 eggs of which, depending upon prevailing conditions, a greater or lesser percentage will see the light of day, and fewer still, maturity. Should we rejoice or feel sympathy for the male of the species, for he is outnumbered and has many wives?

Somewhere in the next few miles above the Whitikau outlet, above the Fence Pool, above the reaches and runs which border the Rangipo Farm, through into the almost unexplored gorge, the remainder will stop, will make their redd in a shallow, pebbled bed and deposit their ova and milt.

Throughout the autumn, the winter and on into the early spring, the cycle continues, and for the angler who knows not only the thrill of a sudden strike but can appreciate the splendour which surrounds him, there can be no greater privilege than to fish the greatest river of them all, the Tongariro.

Let's fish it, shall we? But first you'll need some tackle and a little casting practice.

CHAPTER 2

TACKLE

TIME WAS, and not too long ago either, when an angler had a different rod for every day of the week, another for every stream within a radius of a hundred miles, and a few spares to be brought out and expounded upon at great length when the bottle of Scotch diminished to a level somewhere below the distillery's brand name.

There were massive three-piece 14-footers of split cane weighing an ounce a foot, reserved, it must be said, for rivers such as the Tongariro, and where distance casting was imperative. Beautiful they were too, built by craftsmen for the powerful of wrist and forearm or those fortunate enough to be blessed with exquisite timing. Awesome and completely beyond the frail, the novice and the lady angler (I have an aversion to both "fisherwoman" and "anglerette"), you either swung the rod or it swung you. The essence of perfect timing in the hands of an expert, they were a calamity in the making for ordinary mortals. You held 90 feet of beautifully poised horizontal silk line on your final back-cast, or you flailed the water to a froth behind you. To some, a wand designed to let a line caress the water; to the majority, a telegraph pole with powerline attached.

Odds were even that the compleat angler would then display in descending order, a Wye of 12 feet, a 10 foot six inch Crown Houghton, a 9 foot 6 inch Pope two-piece, a 9 foot Knockabout and a brace of dry-fly rods, of lesser length, one of which would be a Koh-i-noor. Chances were good that in a weak moment you had bought, or more luckily had had bequeathed you, a Joe Frost Tonga and, at some time or another Geoff Sanderson had extolled the virtues of a Walker-Bampton.

I know this to be true, for at some time or another during my years of fishing I have owned them all, often four or five at a time. The nearest and dearest in my life was remembered in my last will and testament under the heading "Rods and Tackle" (number two in my esteem was the recipient of "Golf Clubs and Accessories" and anyone further down the list was, in the modern idiom, fresh out of luck).

These superbly crafted rods, with matching reels and lines, absorbed all my earnings, and, if realised upon, would have gone far toward repaying the National Debt. I still have some of them—indeed, I couldn't bear to part with them—but no longer do they accompany me to the Tongariro.

It was all of fifteen years ago that the first fibreglass fly rods were introduced to this country, and like the majority of fishermen at that time, I looked, felt, swung and did not buy. Unlike the split-cane, which gave action from the top right through to the butt, these early models were extremely whippy in the top section and as stiff as a broom handle in the lower. There was no rapport between man and rod. The new equipment was only a fraction of the price of good cane, but casting was a chore to be endured. Youngsters with exuberant ambition and limited pocket money bought them, the serious angler remained aloof.

There followed, however, a slow but decided improvement in both the action and variety of fibreglass rods, and even the confirmed split-cane fanatic was heard to pass grudging approval of those of new, light, hollow construction.

It was with the introduction to the New Zealand market of the Fenwick Feralite models FF98 and FF112 that many of us finally surrendered and made our first glass purchase. Fast in action, which means that only the last few inches of the tip worked whilst casting, they weighed only $4\frac{5}{8}$ oz and $5\frac{1}{8}$ oz respectively for their lengths of 9 feet and 9 feet 3 inches. Immensely powerful, they projected a line a country mile with a modicum of effort. Better still, they were half the cost of a top-price cane and one's elderly maiden aunt could wield them all day without being troubled by her tennis elbow which had been plaguing her since 1919.

They had other advantages, and not inconsiderable ones: despite being hollow they were nearly indestructible, they required the barest minimum of maintenance and they weren't affected by climatic changes.

Since that time New Zealand manufacturers have gone in for their production on a massive scale and the results are, depending upon the price tag, consistent and excellent.

My own preference now leans to a pair of 9-foot slow action glass rods given to me by my regular client and good friend Captain Stu

Apte of Florida. Made by Scientific Anglers in the United States, the "feel" and action of this model is throughout its entire length and, providing one waits sufficiently long on the backcast, which after the Feralite I found difficult to do for a while, a long cast is possible without undue force.

One still sees the 14-footers on the river, and the chances are, my novice, that if you do, they will be cast by someone who has a lot to teach you if you will but stand and watch him a while.

One particularly brash youth will long have cause to remember an incident on the Major Jones pool only last April. This lad is a regular visitor from the Capital and, though a barely average caster, considers himself in the top flight. Fishing down in front of him I struck a fish opposite the last big boulder on the far bank, and whilst retrieving line at a fast clip after the initial run, I was approached with the comment, "Have you seen the bloody great rod the silly old —— behind me is using?" I indicated that I had, at the same time wishing I had more room to manoeuvre as he was now at my shoulder. "He doesn't have to cast," he said, "he just rests the tip on the far bank and pays out line."

"Oh, he can cast all right," I replied, whilst gradually getting my fish under control. Only the previous day I had watched the "old ——" ease his way through the same pool behind me and take four to my two.

"Why the heck he doesn't light a fire with it and buy a fibreglass, I don't know," was know-it-all's retort, and he proceeded to start casting. I eased a fresh run 5-pounder on to the bank and indicated to them that I should rest a while and they should move on through.

From the identical position in which I had struck my fish, the elderly angler took another. Rather more quickly than I had, he beached it, we both admired it, and he moved back in. Five yards further down, what proved to be a big jack took hold, and in typical fashion, sulked on the bottom shaking his great head in disbelief. Disbelief showed on the face of the young know-it-all too, for hadn't he already fished that water? Ten minutes later the jack joined the other in the shade of the big log.

So it proceeded to the denouement. By the time they were under the wires at the far end of the pool, the score was: Expert Old Timer, 5; Know-it-all, 0.

The lad was first to return up the bank. "He really can cast, can't

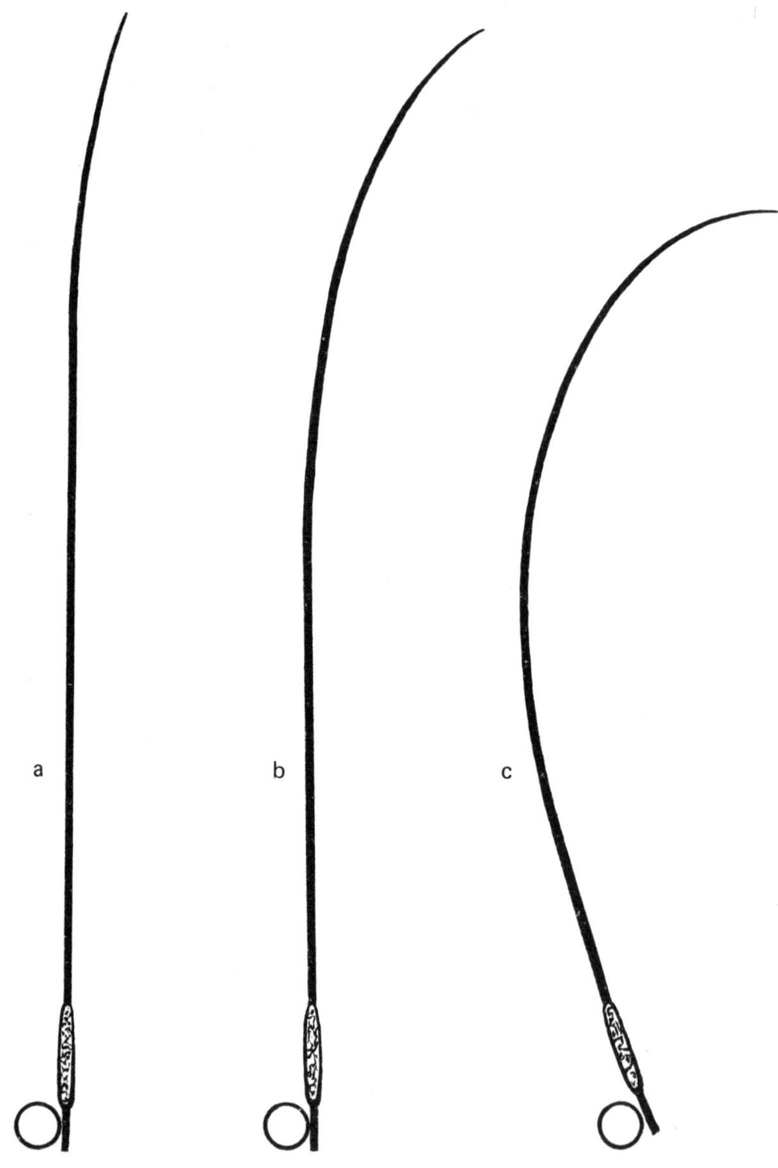

ROD ACTION

Diagram depicting the three basic actions of rods:—

(a) A stiff or fast-action rod suitable for an angler who is a powerful caster or of an excitable disposition. Only the tip of the rod works throughout the cast.

(b) A medium-action rod with the butt section remaining relatively firm during the cast.

(c) A soft or slow-action rod with the bow extending from the tip right down the grip. Excellent equipment for those anglers with good, slow timing.

he?" I enquired, trying desperately to restrain a grin. Perhaps I didn't succeed, for there was no reply.

In selecting a rod for a new chum intent upon fishing the Tongariro, I look now for a fibreglass one in the middle to upper-price bracket, approximately 9 feet in length and with enough backbone to make casting easy with a fast sinking line. If your temperament is inclined to be fiery, if you do things in a rush, the odds are that you will require a stiff-actioned rod. If, on the other hand, you habitually take things quietly and methodically, the slower-action and more supple rod will probably be your choice. This is not a rule of thumb however, and if there is doubt in your mind, take along a friend who knows both you and his fishing well, as an adviser.

Lines

It is under this heading that I find recommendations more difficult than in any other tackle requirement.

Were you going to fish in no waters other than the Tongariro, the selection would be simple in the extreme. Get the fastest sinking line available and proceed to do your damnedest. As easy as that.

But you'll also want to sample the joys which other waters have to offer—strange indeed is the sportsman whose eyes do not light up and whose heart does not beat faster at the thought of new and unexplored territory. Naturally, then, your extra-fast sinking line is going to be a liability on small streams whose beds are covered with snags of all descriptions. Similarly, there's nothing more frustrating than to be sinking your fly when trout are rising all around you, taking naturals on the surface.

Probably no other facet of fly fishing equipment has revealed greater advances in technical achievement than the casting line over the past few years.

When I first became interested in freshwater fishing, lines were almost exclusively made of silk. I have already recounted my early experience with one which had either grown weary or had been sadly neglected. These lines were a source of constant worry. Not only did they require cleaning and drying following the day's fishing, but at regular intervals throughout the season a dressing of one form or another had to be applied. They all sank, which was fine when the fish were keeping to the bottom, but should a rise occur you had to apply a floatant solution. You could then place a wager that by the time this was attended to, the fish would have returned to the

Whitikau Stream at junction with Tongariro River.

bottom. It was then the devil of a job to make the line sink again. Strong men have been known to crumble on such occasions.

When we compare these with their modern counterparts we find we are more than fortunate. By a process of trapping air cells in the coating of a fly line, it can be made to float without dressing throughout its lifetime. Similarly, varying densities can be achieved in sinking lines so that, depending upon the type of water to be fished and the habits of the fish therein, the perfect article for the job is available. A fairly regular rub-down with a damp rag to remove any clinging pumice accumulation is all the attention necessary.

Spawning trout during their upstream run are for the most part not interested in feeding. Before leaving the lake they have gorged themselves in anticipation of the long trek ahead of them, and live almost exclusively off their body fat during their time in the rivers. The reason we catch a few of the many thousands is that we annoy them into a spontaneous snap at something which has been drawn almost across their noses. Lying on, or extremely close to the bottom of the riverbed as they do, in wet fly or downstream fishing one must select the line which will take the fly down to the fish quickly.

In heavy and deep waters such as one encounters in the Tongariro, the fastest sinking fly line available should be utilised, and I recommend for the beginner, a weight-forward extra-fast sinking type. The double tapered line has the advantage of being reversible, but doesn't "shoot" as well or as far.

The experienced sportsman will either select this weight-forward or the line used for casting extreme distances—the shooting taper, more often referred to as a shooting head. Definitely not the line for those new to the game, it enables water to be fished which is often out of range for other fishermen. Consisting of only 30 feet of high-density line, it is backed up with 100 feet of 18-24 lb monofilament which is, in turn, attached to the normal braided backing, so as to comfortably fill the spool of the reel.

Having false-cast the head a yard or so through the tip ring of the rod on the penultimate cast, the line is then shot and with only the extremely light monofilament to pull behind it, distance is easily attained.

The best modern aid for the shooting-head exponent. The stripping basket is the ultimate for this type of fishing. Monofilament or floating backing lies coiled in the basket ready to be shot with only one or two false casts of the shooting head.

As we have mentioned, different waters require different lines, and fishing downstream with a lure or wet fly on some of the smaller rivers and streams, a fast sinking line (as distinct from the extra fast high-density product) should suffice. The line will still get down to the fish but will be less likely to pick up snags as it swings across the current.

Of latter years I have had tremendous enjoyment fishing the Tauranga-Taupo, Waimarino and Waiotaka streams with a nymph fished upstream and across, and my choice for this type of fishing is a comparatively new line aptly described as a wet-tip. Weight-forward in construction, it is a conventional floating line with exactly 10 feet of sinking tip to which the leader and nymph are attached. Nymphing requires more concentration than any type of fishing with the exception of dry fly work. Having made the cast above the fish, the undressed nymph proceeds to sink and the line must be watched intently as it floats back towards the angler. Upon the slightest check to its flow through the current, the strike must be made quickly and decisively or the trout will have rejected the fly.

Many skilful sportsmen I know still prefer the complete floating line for this type of work claiming, justifiably, that they can keep the end of the line under scrutiny throughout its journey and thus notice more readily any interruption to its path. In an extremely shallow glide or run, I agree, but in the deeper holes and pools, I am convinced that the wet tip allows the nymph to descend further and is, of a consequence, at a position closer to the streambed where the fish are lying. My claim therefore is that I shall, perhaps, miss more strikes, but shall have more fish attack my nymph.

The wet tip, too, is the finest line I know for fishing to smelting fish around the lake shore and at stream mouths during November, December and January. Smelt are not *on* the surface at this time but *under* it, and the wet tip approximates the depth almost to an exactitude. If the reader is an enthusiast at smelting time, and has not yet added one of these lines to his tackle, I recommend them to his attention. I am completely convinced that they catch more fish at this time of year and are invaluable when fishing weed beds in lakes which have this problem.

There are few areas in the Taupo neighbourhood which lend themselves to outstanding dry fly fishing, with the possible exception of the Waikato River. However, the South Island is world-renowned for its free-rising browns and rainbows, and there are literally hundreds of streams in the North Island where excellent sport can be obtained by fishing in this manner. Should there be waters in your immediate area which offer trout eager to rise for naturals, the chances are good that a replica in a dry-fly will yield good sport. For this, of course, a floating line is a must, and with the modern trend away from the green colour of previous years, this type of fishing is becoming easier for those whose eyesight is not what it used to be. It is still a decided advantage to be able to see a no. 12 or 14 fly bobbing down the stream towards you, but the new lines of orange or white make the job of striking just that much easier.

It follows, therefore, that according to the waters you are likely to fish, there is a specific line these days to suit your purpose. They are not inexpensive, but a tapered line will cast better and give you far more pleasure to use than one of level construction.

The rod and line you purchase are the two most essential pieces of tackle in your fishing equipment. It is far better to lighten your pocket considerably upon these two items at the expense of a few dozen gaudy flies.

Reels

"I'm long overdue for a new reel, Tony," remarked a young local to me just the other day. "What sort should I buy?"

"Let's have a look at the tackle you're using now," I suggested. He produced a fine Feralite 116 rod and a reel which, at a glance, I guessed to be a Hardy St John. It wasn't new, obviously, but having owned one myself for over twenty years I was surprised to find that he wished to replace it.

"But that's a fine reel you have there," I told him. "Can't see why you'd want to change."

"Wind it and you'll see," he replied. It was no mean task to get the handle working the spool within the drum, so I asked him if he'd dropped it on a rock at any recent stage.

"Not to my knowledge," he said. I took the reel apart and gazed at an accumulation of sand, grit, and dried-up oil that had been there for donkey's ages.

"I don't think you need a new reel," I said. "What you do need is a lesson in looking after your equipment." Within ten minutes we had removed the offending garden of debris the reel had accumulated over a long period. Kerosene did the trick. Then an application of reel grease to pawl and check, and the spare spring which these reels always have was slipped into place. That reel ran like a new one from the first touch on the handle.

"What were you going to spend on a new reel?" I asked him.

"Perhaps twenty bucks or so".

"Go and buy yourself a new line," I said. "This one is shocking—but make sure you keep out a dollar for a bottle of kerosene and some lubricant. And use them. Frequently."

He looked a little abashed, but took off for the tackle shop with a whistle.

The purchase of a fly-reel is not a particularly difficult task. It is wise, however, to ensure that the reel will balance your rod. These days, the great majority of reels are manufactured with the lighter fibreglass rods in mind, and it is rarely that the very heavy models of yesteryear are encountered. If your finances permit, endeavour to find a good English make, around 3¾ inches in diameter and capable of carrying at least 100 yards of backing plus the fly line. Chances are, it will then have a spare spring and pawl built into the drum and, more important, the spool will fit exactly into the drum. Many of the less expensive makes look fine but after some use they're inclined to spread, allowing the line or backing to be nipped between the two components. Nothing can damage your good line as quickly as this.

The Americans make some excellent reels, but these are not readily available in this country, and import duty would probably make them too expensive in any case. Whichever reel you do select, do maintain it better than my young friend did.

Flies

Put a dozen anglers together, open the second bottle of Scotch, mention the lure you have used with success only that day, and you have an argument on your hands. Should you be mathematically inclined and be in a fit state to make notations, you will probably count no fewer than three dozen favourites, all different, from among the assembled throng. Some will, moreover, subscribe to the adage of "big fly, big fish" while others will claim success for patterns tied on a no. 8 or even a no. 10 hook.

The ancient fellow in the corner will advance the theory that the trout he took back in the thirties on a Turkey and Red will still succumb to it. The excited young man by the fire, who is having difficulty in focusing, will produce from his pocket a gaudy, red, orange, purple and yellow monstrosity which a half-blind gourmand of a fish had amazingly taken in the Island Pool on the previous day. The scholarly gentleman in glasses with the "more-water-in-mine-please" approach will advance his preference for a lightly-dressed Parson's Glory on a no. 6 hook.

Half an hour of this and the new boy to the game will be sufficiently confused to turn a deaf ear to the lot and take three rapid swallows as a prelude to refilling his glass.

When trout were first introduced to New Zealand, fishermen delved deep into long-neglected cabin trunks which relatives had brought out from England and Scotland, discovered long-unused flyboxes, and proceeded to catch fish on most of the salmon and sea-run trout patterns found therein. These worked, and worked well, but the New Zealander is by nature an inventive fellow, and it wasn't long before flies made of readily available New Zealand feathers were being tied.

One of the first birds to have both his dignity and his life-expectancy upset was the native bittern or matuku; his distinctive plumage yielded many flies and the flies yielded many fish. So popular was the matuku that it was feared he would become extinct, and the ungainly bird was finally granted a reprieve when he found a place on the strictly-protected list.

The kiwi feathers too were much prized, and though more difficult to obtain because of the bird's nocturnal habits, it became necessary to elevate him too, to the ranks of the inviolate. Wild animals, birds, dogs, blonde children, roosters—none was safe—and gradually generally-accepted patterns peculiar to this country were introduced.

It is my previously stated contention that the trout which enter our river system are not feeding fish, and are in the rivers purely and simply for their fishy love-life. With the exception of an odd kelt or resident fish, I have yet to find evidence of a recent meal in the stomach of any fish I have taken and dressed on the riverbank.

Thus I am not as adamant as many fishing folk I know, when it comes to fly selection. I do feel however that certain flies produce that spontaneous snapping reaction from trout better than others in certain conditions of light and water colour.

I don't expect my selection to meet with universal approval; indeed, I would be disappointed if it did, for much good argument and discussion would be lost if everyone were to agree.

For what they are worth, then, I offer some patterns which have yielded consistently well for both my clients and myself over the past few years whilst river fishing.

Water clear, day bright: Red Setter, Mallard (Widgeon) (yellow body), Grey Rabbit (yellow body). Hook sizes 6 and 8.
Water clear, day overcast: Red Setter, Mrs Simpson (red body), Grey Rabbit (orange body), Hamill's Killer. Hook sizes 6 and 8.
Water cloudy, day bright: Grey Rabbit (red body), Maribou King, Hairy Dog (red or green body) Hook size 4.
Water cloudy, day overcast: Hairy Dog (red body) Kilwell No. 2 (red body) Turkey and Red. Hook size 2.

Monofilament

Quite clearly the least important section of your tackle comes under this heading. However, it is a necessary adjunct and, depending upon your choice of brand, can give you heartburn or satisfaction.

All spools of monofilament are marked with the breaking strain, but I should be much happier were they to disclose the knot strength as well. Many types, say of 9 pounds, would no doubt withstand a straight pull of that pressure, but tie a knot from fly line to leader, or from leader to fly, and they become incredibly weakened.

Tell me an experience more frustrating than to have cast long and hard to unresponsive fish and, upon finally securing a strike, to leave the hook in the trout's mouth through no other reason than that the breaking strain at the knot was far below expectancy.

Of late I have used nothing other than a German nylon which, though more expensive by a few cents than others on the market, seems almost as strong at the knot as anywhere else throughout its length. When all's said and done, from a 50-yard reel, seventeen casts of nine feet in length can be fashioned at a cost of less than five cents apiece. Monofilament does deteriorate fairly rapidly, so when you hang up your rod until next season, throw away those partly-used spools and even the ones which still contain a full length. (In case you wonder, I do not have shares in a German monofilament producing company, nor do I own a tackle shop.)

As with flies, fishermen will always find occasion to argue about the length of leader required in different waters. The theory I hold to, because it seems logical, states that the clearer and shallower the water is, the longer and finer should be the leader. For nymph fishing on the Waiotaka I often utilise one of 12 feet in three sections adjoined with blood knots and the tippet having a breaking strain of no more than 4 pounds. Conversely, on the Tongariro, because I wish to sink my fly as quickly as possible in deep, heavy and often discoloured water, I have sometimes cut back to no more than 4 feet 6 inches of 7½ pound test.

One further rule which is more often than not neglected: having caught a fish, it is of paramount importance that you remove the fly, snip off the half-inch of kinked nylon at the tip and re-tie the fly. Especially does this hold good when the tippet you are using is particularly fine.

Waders

"P.S.: Can you please supply us with waders for our river fishing whilst in New Zealand? I take size 14 and my wife needs size 4½B."

So end many letters I receive each year from overseas fishermen whom I shall be guiding later. They are naturally reluctant to add the not inconsiderable weight and cost to their baggage, especially when travelling by air. (In passing, it is undeniable that just as Americans have the biggest automobiles, the biggest skyscrapers and the biggest incomes, American men also have the greatest grip on Mother Earth.)

I make the necessary reservation in my diary and add: "Mr—, size 12 waders; Mrs—, size 5", for these are the largest and smallest made in this country. It is surprising, but they nearly always fit.

To fish the Tongariro satisfactorily, body waders are a must. In making your purchase, remember that the season is now open during the months of winter when you'll need two and sometimes three pairs of socks. Nothing will make feet feel the cold of the river more quickly than waders which leave you no room to wiggle your toes.

Joe Brooks, author and fishing editor of the American *Outdoor Life* magazine, and probably the finest caster of a fly it has been my privilege to guide, described New Zealanders in his article on Tongariro fishing as "lantern-jawed men in black waders moving purposefully through the pool". Possibly the fishing was hard that day, accounting for the expressions, but it is rare to see body waders other than of a coal-black colour. Heavier in texture than most of the overseas pairs, they have the advantage in warmth, and probably do not puncture as easily from blackberry thorns and fellow fishermen's hooks.

The standard waders one finds in tackle shops have a corrugated rubber sole which I consider to be completely unsuitable for the Tongariro. With a riverbed often covered with weed-covered rocks, all of which seem to be round, all of which seem to have been covered with grease, and all of which seem determined to move or roll under your feet, some additional aid to wading is prudent. When all is said and done, the first time you fall over in really heavy water might well be the last.

Certainly the most effective is the de-luxe wader which sports a thick felt sole. These are a splendid aid, and enable the angler to move confidently through the most difficult pools. They have one disadvantage however: the pumice nature of our country has an abrasive effect and, despite the thickness of the felt, it is unlikely that the soles will stand up for more than one season if you are a busy fisherman. Fitting a new pair is the devil of a job too, and a pair of good thick felt soles are expensive. Some fellows I know have experimented with heavy carpeting attached to the boot soles with epoxy resin. These seem to work well.

If you decide against the felt or carpet for reasons of expense or time involved, do at least spend a few cents on a pair of heavy heel-plates. Though not the ultimate, they'll help you over some of the more slippery surfaces, and will at some stage save you a ducking, which by bitter experience, both literally and metaphorically, I know to be far from pleasant.

Accessories

I make a point of meeting each new client on the evening before starting our fishing trip. The reasons are many. I want to get to know him a little, to find out the type of fishing he prefers, to be able to tell my wife Jo whether he likes tea or coffee in the thermos flasks and, very importantly, to check the tackle he has brought with him. Should we have been corresponding before his arrival he will have had my recommendations and there will be no problem. Many however have said, simply, "Let's go and fish New Zealand", and here the trouble starts. Proudly he displays the four rods he has protected with his life throughout the hazards of 10,000 miles of air travel. Two of them will be excellent for herring fishing from a pier, and the other two will suffice to tame a blue marlin in the Bay of Islands in twenty minutes flat.

An assortment of a dozen reels may reveal one which has sufficient size for a fly line sans backing, and the remaining half ton of equipment contains a pair of folding nets, two thousand spoons and assorted hardware all fitted with treble hooks (illegal in the area), a lead-head priest for the quick despatch of his first 12-pounder, and

Poutu Pool.

dozens of plastic boxes displaying flies, lures, nymphs and replicas of grasshoppers, crickets, worms and frogs. To cap it all off there are the inevitable salmon-egg imitations and some cheese-flavoured marshmallows which "proved deadly on a little lake in Northern California only last summer".

One has to be gentle at times like this. It is distressing in the extreme to watch a grown man cry, and some approach this state when you inform them that practically all the tackle they have prepared so lovingly over the past several months is eminently unsuitable for local conditions.

The point I'm trying to make here is that providing you have the correct tackle for the water you want to fish, there's no reason to weigh yourself down with unnecessary paraphernalia.

Additional to the rod, reel, line, monofilament in two or three assorted breaking strains, flies to suit the day, and your waders, you need only a pair of clippers or scissors, a wading staff, if you like to use a store-bought one instead of a convenient branch, your lunch and your patience. And if you haven't got patience, nine times out of ten, you should have stayed at home anyway.

CHAPTER 3

CASTING

THE GOLF PRO, when faced with a pupil who has never swung a club before, will start the first lesson by saying, "If your hands are in correct position and have firm control on the grip of the shaft, you've got much more chance of building a good swing". So it is with a fly rod but, unlike golf, so far as the grip is concerned we have only one hand to worry about.

Novices at both golf and fishing are so determined that the thing is not going to get away from them that their knuckles show white with the strain. A smooth swing or a smooth cast are impossible under such conditions.

Take hold of the rod lightly with an even pressure of all fingers, and thumb placed along the top of the cork. Many fine casters I know allow the thumb to ride over the grip a little, and if this feels more comfortable, by all means adopt it.

Good casting is based on three movements, pickup, backcast, and forward cast, all related and each dependent upon the other. A correct pickup will allow a good backcast, and this having been achieved, a good forward throw should follow.

If you have access to a floating line which comes off the water much more readily than its sinking counterpart, practise with that until you are confident enough to begin work with the sinker. Pull about 30 feet of line from the reel and allow it to fall to the ground. Begin false casting, allowing two or three feet of line to be taken through the guides by the action of the rod. Once the 30 feet is on the water, lift the rod to a position midway between horizontal and vertical, then extend the casting arm outward toward the fly. A smooth but firm upward movement of the arm and flip of the wrist will start the line on its backward journey. Ideally, the tip of the rod will be pointing to about the 2 o'clock position at the completion of the backswing, by which time the line will be straightening out behind you. At this point, it is essential to hesitate until the lagging

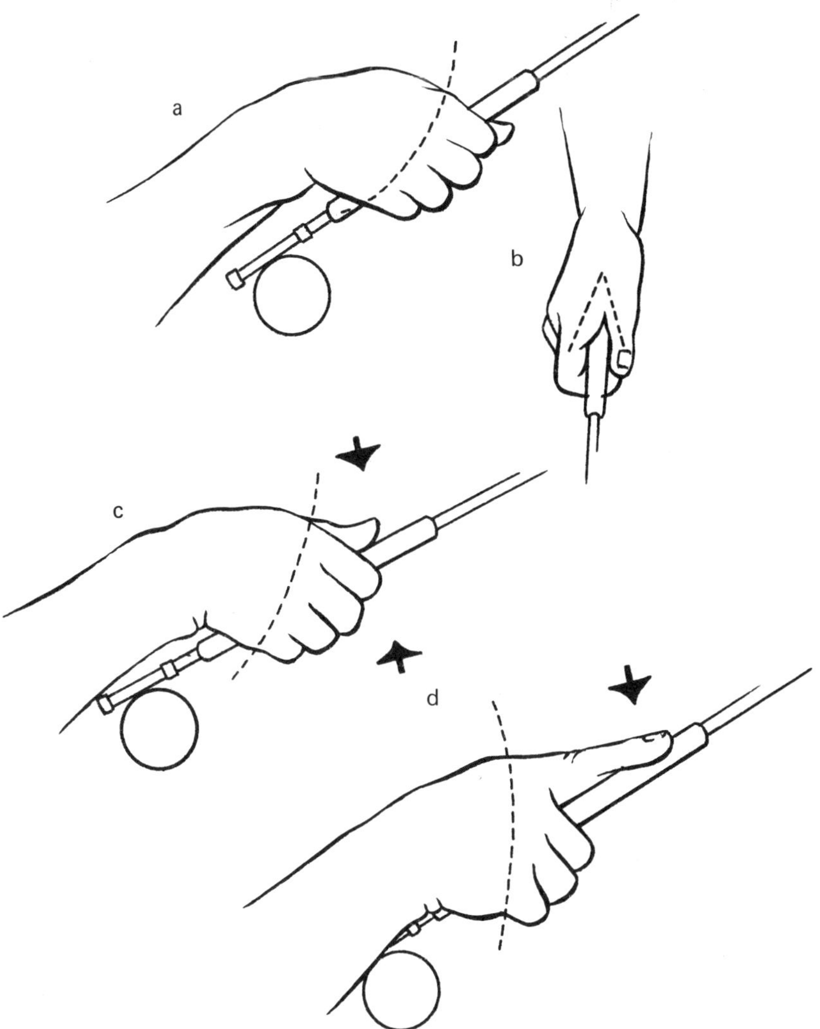

THREE ACCEPTABLE GRIPS FOR CASTING, SHOWING

(a) The thumb overriding the cork.
(b) The vee formed by index finger and thumb pointing directly towards the butt of the rod.
(c) The most widely used grip with thumb along the top of the handle.
(d) The author's rather more unusual grip adopted as a check to overswinging on the backcast.

leader and fly have caught up and passed the line, and all have attained the horizontal position.

Most beginners are too impatient to begin the forward throw, and try and force the line back against its own backward momentum. They're cracking it like a stockwhip and nothing breaks flies off leaders so quickly. If you're in doubt about just where the line is, turn your head and watch its path until you see it straighten. To start the forward cast, allow the elbow to drop a few inches and, aiming for a spot about 45 degrees above the horizontal, take the rod forward by snapping the wrist and extending the arm. The cast should be made, and the line shot, from the 2 o'clock position. Should the line be held too long before release, say, until 12 o'clock, a downward thrust from the rod tip will not only reduce the length of the throw, but also will result in a birdsnest of line, leader and fly hitting the water all at the same time.

THE BASIC CAST

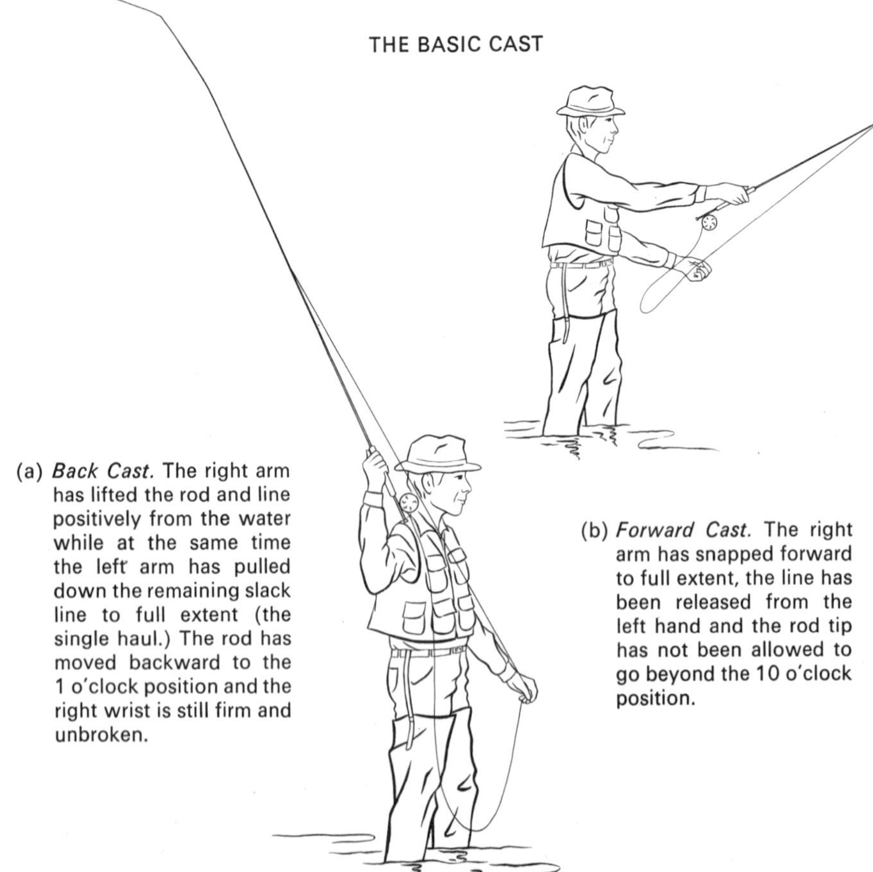

(a) *Back Cast.* The right arm has lifted the rod and line positively from the water while at the same time the left arm has pulled down the remaining slack line to full extent (the single haul.) The rod has moved backward to the 1 o'clock position and the right wrist is still firm and unbroken.

(b) *Forward Cast.* The right arm has snapped forward to full extent, the line has been released from the left hand and the rod tip has not been allowed to go beyond the 10 o'clock position.

Try getting good timing by false-casting about 30 feet of line backward and forward until at all times you know where the line is. It's tiring, but before long, you'll be adding 20 or 30 feet to the original length and you'll be doing it easily.

Wind is one factor most fly casters dread more than any other element, and often the comment is heard, "I've just packed it in. That wind's blowing the fly back in my face". Unless it is blowing at gale force or storm strength straight at you, wind should not spoil your fun too much, provided you have learned to make the straightforward cast we have just discussed. Into wind, allow the rod to be taken well back behind you, maintaining the line at the usual parallel. On the forward cast, however, drop your elbow really low and allow the rod to continue on past its normal finishing position of 10 o'clock until it's only a foot or so off the water. These dual efforts will enable the fly to be shot out low to the water and under much of

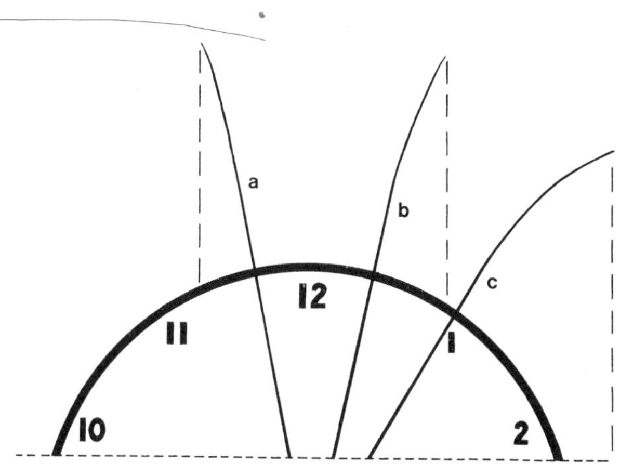

THE CLOCK

A backswing which is too restricted as in (a) above has not allowed the rod to begin its action.
In (b) only the first few inches of the tip have begun to work, and the result will be a downward thrust and a short, heavily presented cast.
In (c) the full action of a medium-action rod is being brought into play enabling a long, powerful cast to be made.

Note: When using the double-haul cast it is possible to take the rod back to the 2 o'clock position for extra distance, although it should be noted that when the butt is pointing to 1 o'clock the tip has actually moved past 2 o'clock.

the wind. It's a cast which requires practice, but in a country like ours it's a valuable aid to the enjoyment of your fishing.

Most right-handed casters can handle the wind which comes at them from left to right, but when it buffets from the opposite quarter they are really in trouble. Mentally they see that fly describing an arc on the wind and coming back to be firmly buried in the nape of the caster's neck.

These conditions are overcome by taking the backcast up and over the left shoulder and timing the cast as you would for the normal delivery. In this manner, the line is always a little downwind of you and when brought back, once again over the left shoulder, is comfortably clear of a protruding ear.

A back wind can cause troubles, especially when it is blowing really hard, by knocking down your backcast past the horizontal.

CASTING INTO WIND

The illustration shows the finishing position of the cast when the angler is trying to push line into a strong wind. Take the back cast a little further than on the basic cast. As the line reaches the horizontal, drop the right elbow at least six inches and on the forward cast allow the rod to continue well past its normal finishing position until it is only a foot or so clear of the water. The line will then have shot through low and under much of the wind.

I've seen fellows barb twenty flies in a day on this wind, especially if the terrain behind them is slightly elevated. Not only does it spoil a day's fishing for them, but they have wasted a lot of precious time and are a few dollars out of pocket. But this tail wind can be made to help if you'll let it.

Just as when we were casting into wind we allowed a slightly fuller backcast and brought the rod down within a foot of the water on the follow through, so does the reverse apply in this instance. Shorten both the length of line and your backswing, and on the forward cast stop the rod at about the 11 o'clock position aiming as high as 45 degrees above the water. The line will shoot out high on the wind, gaining momentum both from the cast and the assistance of the wind.

I find a modified version of the double haul particularly helpful where I am striving to cover an extremely wide pool. As the fly is leaving the water for the backcast, pull the line quite firmly downward and sideways as the rod moves backward to the 2 o'clock position of the backcast.

As the line is then moving out to the horizontal plane behind, allow the left hand to rise to a point immediately under the butt-ring of the rod and, to begin the forward cast, pull down sharply on the line. This has the effect of developing far greater speed than the rod-tip itself can impart, and will assist in an improved casting potential.

It will be noticed from the illustration (p. 36) that when a shooting-head line is used with the double haul, the rod is stopped in its forward cast position at a point around 45 degrees above the horizontal from the water and not at the lower position normally used in casting the weight-forward or double-taper line. Try, too, to start the cast from the 2 o'clock position of the backcast with a snap of the wrist and forearm as if hammering a nail into a wall which is facing you. Should the release of the line be made later in the forward cast, say at 12 o'clock, it is almost impossible to stop the rod at the required 10 o'clock angle and the result will be a downward throw and a sloppy short cast.

One word of warning here: when practising the double haul on your front lawn or on the water, I do recommend using a fly which has been barbed. The final, downward pull with the left hand has the effect of bringing the fly through lower than is normally the case when the single haul only is being used, and it is always embarrassing and often painful to have to ask a neighbour to remove a no. 4 Hairy Dog from the back of one's neck.

THE DOUBLE HAUL—FOR EXTRA DISTANCE

(a) Begin the back cast with a strong uplift of the right arm and a corresponding downward pull of the left arm. This constitutes a single haul.
(b) As the rod moves back to the 1 o'clock position (2 o'clock for maximum length of cast) allow the left arm to follow up and across the body.
(c) At the precise moment that the line has straightened out behind the angler, the left arm once again pulls down to the same position it had gained in Fig (a).
(d) The right arm snaps forward and the cast is made.

HAMMER THAT NAIL

When making a normal forward cast try to imagine that you are using a hammer to drive a nail into a wall in front of you at eye level or slighty higher. This will eliminate any tendency to let the wrist break forward, resulting in a downward, short throw.

A friend of mine has good cause to remember this advice. Fishing at Cattle Rustlers' pool one day a couple of years ago, he was continually barbing hooks on the high stone bank behind him. Wondering what was happening to his backcast, he decided to look around and watch the action of the line and fly. This time all was in order and he began his cast while still looking backward. A split-second later he was the shocked recipient of a Red Setter which had become firmly and irretrievably embedded in the very centre of his nose.

A tentative probe through crossed eyes convinced him that he would have to seek help from another source, and every angler at the poolside had a go at it. Bert didn't find the situation at all amusing, but all who came to assist appeared to be shaking with ill-concealed mirth, thus rendering the extraction all the more improbable. The fly was still firmly attached, bushy tail upward, eye exactly midway between his nostrils, when he started the long walk back to the Major Jones swingbridge. To this day he swears he met no fewer than fifty anglers along the trail, all of whom expressed consternation, but all of whom continued their journey chortling helplessly. Halfway over the bridge and within sight of his vehicle, he was appalled to find a family of young children advancing from the other side. They stopped, they stared, and in the manner of children everywhere, they commenced to hoot with delight, their glee at his embarrassment following him until he fell into the car a beaten and embittered man.

His rout was complete when upon entering the doctor's surgery he was faced with a waitingroom full to overflowing with patients. Some smiled: some smirked; others, less inhibited, laughed outright, and within ten seconds the whole room was shaking. Enter nurse to find the cause of the disturbance in the usually churchlike atmosphere, and she too departed with tears rolling down her cheeks to call Doctor. Bert is adamant that the good man giggled like a schoolgirl at her first dance while performing the operation.

It is not strange that I have never again seen Bert look backward to see what is happening to his line, but he's one of the finest New Zealand-born casters I know. For the beginner, I encourage the habit, but if you are an absolute tyro, do take the point from the hook during practice.

Every so often you may find that undergrowth immediately behind and deep or fast water right in front of you, presents a difficulty in fishing to a likely-looking lie. Joe Brooks, who is a master of the art, showed me how to overcome this problem with what he calls his change-of-direction cast. We were fishing the Rabbiters' block on the Waiotaka Stream, and the nymph he was presenting so beautifully upstream and across at a 45-degree angle had already taken three good fish.

It was then that we saw a rainbow about 50 feet ahead of us which made the others look like minnows. Joe whistled through his teeth and said, "You could throw a saddle on that baby and ride him home. He's so big he wouldn't even feel the strain".

We had our problems however, for throughout the next 20 yards of the stream, trees and undergrowth overhung the water leaving only a narrow gap which, unfortunately did not lead to the fish. Joe studied the position for a good minute before he spoke. "I think a change-of-direction cast will let me get that guy, Tony."

I watched, fascinated, as Joe false-cast the line through that narrow gap, increasing the length of the cast each time until he assessed he had sufficient out to make his final throw. I remember thinking "That's surely going to land up in the bushes on the opposite side of the stream to the fish".

As he started the forward throw Joe turned his torso in the direction of the trout and rolled his wrist to the right. If he'd taken it

Joy on the upper river.

and placed it, he couldn't have done better. That nymph landed 8 feet beyond the fish, caught the eddy which led to the lie and must have bumped him on the nose.

I watched the line as it came back down the current, but Joe was quicker to the sensation of the strike, and up went his tip. It came down even faster than he'd struck, there was an eruption of water, and the fight was on. That fish was really offended and decided that aerobatics were the order of the day. Five leaps later and still secure, it turned nasty. Like a streak of lightning it charged upstream and as suddenly reversed, bearing down on a frantically reeling angler as if to knock his feet from under him. Downstream through the shallows it went, through the rapids to the next pool, and in under a bank rife with snags.

Joe followed, reeling in all the time, and with the reluctant victim now on a short line he was able to steer him around an evil manuka branch and out into the centre of the pool. Applying a little more pressure now that the fish was tiring, he gradually worked him into the shallows where I put my hand over his back and lifted him gently to shore.

"That's as good a fight as I've had in a small stream like this," said Joe. "He deserves to be released, but let's weigh him first for the record." Gently we hung him from the scales, $7\frac{3}{4}$ pounds of male rainbow was recorded, the colour-photograph later to appear in *Outdoor Life* magazine was shot, and carefully the trout was slipped back into the pool. "You know," I said as we sat down to a cup of coffee, "I'd have passed up that trout as impossible to cast to."

"The change-of-direction cast, combined with the curve I threw when I turned that wrist over did the trick," he said. "Without the combination, that trout was as safe as he would have been in a sanctuary."

It is through association with the world's best that ordinary mortals are taught the tricks of the trade, and I have learned much through watching and then practising what I have watched. Certainly, I never now decide a trout is safe because of his lie, and the satisfaction of getting a strike from a fish lying in a seemingly hopeless position is worth half a dozen taken the easy way. And even when the fishing is tough, throwing a line a long way and seeing it land right on the riffle of water you have selected for the fly is a joy in itself.

So now you've bought your tackle, you've practised your casting, and though not yet expert you're anxious to have your first day on the river.

Everything's in our favour too. The frost is thawing and the day promises blue skies and no wind. The Tongariro is clear, the fish are running and, to make our joy unconfined, no car is parked at the Dreadnought swingbridge. The Fence, the Sand and the Blue pools are beckoning, and today the guiding is free.

So what are we waiting for? Let's go!

CHAPTER 4

THE FENCE, THE WHITIKAU, THE SAND AND THE BLUE

THE ANCIENT STRUCTURE which crosses the Poutu River just upstream of its confluence with the Tongariro is known as the Dreadnought swingbridge. To the faint of heart and frail of resolution, it is aptly named. Suspended from wire cables, it sways alarmingly the minute the first foot touches it, and the sideways momentum increases with every step. Below, the Poutu rushes headlong as if sensing the imminent meeting and merging of waters with its big sister, and if you suffer from vertigo it is unwise to look downward.

To fish the Fence, the Sand and the Blue pools, however, we'll have to make the crossing and, such is the beauty of them, the promise that lies ahead, this brief flurry of excitement is soon behind us.

Once over, the path forks. To the left, the hundred-yard walk to the junction of the two rivers, the track winding through a dense mass of blackberry bushes, black with ripe fruit in season. Today, only the husks remain and we do not tarry but take the trail which leads straight onward through scattered manuka and pine. Ahead lies a half-hour walk if we move briskly, and perhaps an hour if we prefer to enjoy what surrounds us.

A rabbit, timid of the first intruders of the early morning, bounds to the shelter of his burrow or bush, and the whirring departure of a score of quail follows the first whistle of warning from their sentry. Mindful of the wear to which waders are liable on long walks, and aware too that the sun will soon have warmth to it, we have them slung over our shoulders, and our mounted rods are at the trail position. A small thermos of hot tea each and a packet of sandwiches will keep the wolf from the door during the day, and with their contents gone by the time of our return, our hands will be free to cope with the weight of fish we feel sure we're going to catch.

At the foot of the cliff which guards the western bank of the pool which bears its name, the path circles back and we climb the yellow clay track to the top.

Within a few more paces the transformation of scenery is breathtaking: manuka and blackberry suddenly give way to rolling green pastures dotted with sheep and cattle and, far beyond, the snow-capped peaks of the brother mountains Ruapehu, Ngauruhoe and Tongariro reach for the sky.

It is not merely that I have climbed the cliff that makes me stop here on every trek up-river, for though I love all the area which surrounds the Tongariro, this is to me the most beautiful. To the left, the river itself is visible for a mile upstream, frothing white through the narrow entrance to the Fan Pool, broadening and becoming more quiet as it prepares itself once again for the headlong rush around the Dreadnought corner and into the Cliff. Standing as we are, a hundred feet above the boulder-strewn banks, we can turn and watch her for another half mile as she again becomes wider and moves on through the Boulder Reach before disappearing from view around the bend heading to the Poutu.

Fifteen miles to the south-west the still active volcano of

The Kennedys at their favourite Blue Pool.

Ngauruhoe will, if we are lucky, emit a white mushroom of steam from deep within its crater, while to the east the Kaimanawa Range extends in an unbroken line, tops crested with snow. Men who habitually express themselves in monosyllables and grunts have been known to wax poetical at their first glimpse from this spot, and for those with a love of photography the scene is recaptured for future memories.

But now we must move on, for today is the day of your first trout and we still have a walk ahead of us, albeit an easy one.

We are now on the Rangipo Prison Farm property and a man-made road leads us almost directly towards the Blue Pool. Just how this road came to be formed is a controversial question. Certainly it terminates at a little-used quarry which on occasions is made to yield some particularly unlikely-looking boulders, but most will have it known simply as the Governor General's Road or H.E.'s Road. With a time-consuming itinerary and a love of the upper Tongariro, or so the story goes, someone suggested that the way would be made easy and the fishing time extended if it were possible for him to be driven to the pool of his choice. Decidedly, the road is verboten to the cars of ordinary mortals, but if the Queen's Representative in New Zealand cannot have some privilege beyond the norm, then who can?

Except when weighed down with TV tripods, movie cameras, still cameras, hampers, extra clothing, half a dozen pairs of waders and a spare cabin trunk containing unexposed film, I prefer to walk anyway.

Following the path through the pines and tea-tree, we once again hear the sound of the river and soon the gaps in the trees give us our first glimpse of the Blue Pool. "Majestic" best describes these waters. Moving evenly through the length of the pool, seemingly unhurried yet purposeful, the Blue is one of the most picturesque on the Tongariro. The near bank is golden with lupins, whilst atop the cliff on the far side the trees climb skyward, dwarfing us who stand in their far-reaching shadows. The deepest of blues merge with every toning of green through this stateliest of pools, and it is with some reluctance that we continue further along the trail to the Sand Pool, an easy quarter of a mile onward.

Just as the Blue was majestic, so is the Sand an "intimate" pool. Sheltering under the sheer sandstone cliff after which it was named, it is a place in which to be serene, to be grateful that we are privileged

The serene Sand Pool.

to live in a country which still has surroundings of such loveliness to offer, and to sit a while and gaze, unspeaking. Upstream on the blue-grey boulders close to the water's edge, a blue heron, unaware or disdainful of our presence, stalks some morsel with comic dignity, then becomes transformed with effortless grace as it takes wing.

The Fence

Opposite the Whitikau Stream entrance the track is overgrown and we must pick our way from rock to rock, and around the encroaching scrub until, at last, we see the fence high on the hill above us, indicating we have arrived at our destination, the Fence Pool.

After we have seen the Blue and the Sand it is a little anticlimactic, for it's not a large body of water. To the experienced eye, however, it looks especially designed to hold fish: the narrow entrance to the head of the pool appears to stop abruptly, and the water moves placidly on through the remainder at a slow, even momentum favouring the cliff on the far side. Useless here to cast straight across the river, because the opposite side is only 10 yards removed at the top of the pool, and the quietly moving water will allow the fly to sink rapidly. A 45-degree cast across and down stream should fill the bill nicely.

As in all other waters, we shall start with a couple of short casts into the head of the pool, allowing the natural swing of the current to pull the fly around to the side from which we cast, before retrieving about a foot at a time. In this way, should a trout be lying in the heavy water, we shall have a chance of enticing him to take. So many anglers—often the vastly experienced ones too—rush down to the river, strip off 60 or 70 feet of line and immediately start to cast for the far bank, ignoring water through which their fly will never pass. If the pool has not been fished before your arrival, the chances are that undisturbed fish will be lying in much shallower water than after half a dozen fishermen have waded through. Especially does this hold good first thing in the morning or when the water is discoloured.

Having first thoroughly wet the fly and leader to ensure that it will sink on the first cast, you will start with a 30-foot throw. Two or three of these and then increase the length of cast by about 5 feet. Repeat—5 feet more, and so on until you have reached maximum casting distance. Move down river 6 feet and begin the pattern once again, making sure that if you are first in the pool for the day and intend to fish it more than once, you do not wade too deep.

If you find the fish uncooperative, vary your technique occasionally: try speeding up, or slowing down the pace of your retrieve. Many experts I know give the fly a little twitch as it moves across the current rather than the normal method of letting it float in a "dead" manner. Sometimes, having made your cast, let go additional slack line to assist in sinking the fly. Above all, experiment until you have found the answer to that particular day's requirements.

Generally, I find the middle 20 yards of the Fence Pool the most productive. Throughout the heat of the day the fish seem to be in quite close to the overhanging cliff and a 45-degree cast downstream and the fast release of an additional 10 or 20 feet of slack seems to attract them as well as any other method.

Beyond the tail of this pool there is a long glide which should not be neglected, and I cannot recall an occasion when I have not had at least one strike in it. The trout which bypass the Whitikau Stream have a fairly hard slog from the Sand up to the Fence, and this run seems to provide the first chance they have to rest.

Come to think of it, any water which provides cover either by depth or because of overhanging trees or brush is always worth a flick. Many times over the years I have had a fish accept a fly in a place where a preceding fisherman has not bothered to make a cast.

The day we think we know it all is the day we'll be heading for a fall. It was in this same glide that Jim Conklin, a plastic surgeon from Pittsburgh, gave me one of my lessons. Jim is one of those uncanny anglers who somehow or other will catch a fish in his bathwater. He had taken a splendid 6 lb hen from the Fence Pool but had fished down the glide below with only a touch for his efforts. "Any good going further down, Tony?" he called out.

"No, I don't think so. They won't be lying in that fast water. Why not come on back and we'll see if anyone's working the Sand Pool?"

Now most anglers who employ a guide who has already taken them to a pool which produced fish, would have reeled up and started back. Not so Jim. He moved about four yards further down saying "One last cast here".

I was packing cups into the picnic basket when I heard him yell, "No fish this far down, eh?"

Going like an express train, and obviously hell-bent on creating a new record for the distance back to Lake Taupo was a fish. I scrambled down the bank and hurried to join him, mumbling something about fish that made liars out of guides.

"You win," I told him. "But I'll give you five to one that you don't land him."

Already that trout had stripped off 50 yards of line and, with the heavy current to assist, was making Jim's reel scream like a banshee. I knew, too, that Jim favoured light tippets on his leaders and that the one he was using had a breaking strain of 4 lb. "You're on, in the drink of your choice," he said, but I had the feeling that there was a reserve in his normal confidence.

"You haven't a chance of crossing here," I said, "so somehow or other you've got to stop and turn that fish and regain the line you've lost."

By now Jim was noticeably worried. He knew and I knew that there were 150 yards of backing on the reel, but we doubted that the trout either knew or cared about that. The run had lost its violence and had slowed considerably, but that fish still retained a hatred for any American who dared invade his privacy.

Finally, Jim spoke again through clenched teeth "It's now or never. Look at the backing!"

I looked—and immediately wished I hadn't. Telltale rings of silver had appeared and with every second, more of the naked spool was exposed.

"'Bye, fish," I yelled, and at the same time murmured to Jim "Give him the butt." I needn't have spoken. He had that rod of his bending like a green sapling, held high above his head for extra leverage, and not giving an inch.

How that 4 lb tippet held for so long I shall never know, for he did stop the headlong flight, he did turn the fish towards him once more, and for a dozen seconds he did gain line.

There was a vague commotion on the top of the water away down river and Jim used an expletive which he'd never have used in normal circumstances. . . .

There is a terribly empty moment for both angler and guide when a fight like that has been lost. Winding in nearly 200 yards of line seems to take an eternity, and the silence is broken only by the ratchet of the defeated reel.

Jim looked at the broken tippet and, still saying nothing, fashioned a new one with a blood-knot, tied on another Red Setter, and moved back upstream to the crossing which led to the bank. After a few paces he stopped, turned to me, and said "I've fished for char in the Arctic Ocean, bonefish on the Florida Keys, and marlin off Mexico, but that's the strongest fish, pound for pound, I've ever had on. What do you think it weighed, Tony? Ten pounds? Twelve?"

"Just as likely a 3-pounder foul-hooked in the dorsal fin", I replied, and was forced immediately to take evasive action.

"Wait until I get back home and tell 'em about a rainbow which took out 400 yards of backing at one run and snapped a 12 lb leader like cotton," he said. "You'll have so many people calling you to make bookings from the USA that you'll have to employ another dozen guides and six secretaries."

Well, Jim, you can't be such a good liar as I'd hoped, because I'm still waiting.

The Whitikau

On your way downstream to the Sand Pool from the Fence, we spare some time and a dozen casts for a lie just below the Whitikau Stream entrance. Especially when the Tongariro is running at low level, this run can provide some exciting fishing. The water is heavy, fairly deep and strong, and a fish hooked here is more often landed 100 yards downstream in the Sand Pool than in the area where he was hooked.

The Whitikau is a fantastic spawning stream and presumably the fish which intend running up it to spawn, rest here for a time before entering the shallows. Two large boulders 20 yards apart and only 5 yards from shore indicate the upper and lower reaches of the lie.

The Sand

The Sand Pool isn't the easiest of pools to fish. Where the heavy water enters the head of the pool it forces itself hard against the overhanging cliff and is abruptly turned away. Coming up against a sandbar in the middle of the pool it turns again and forms a swirl which picks up one's line and fly and brings them back under one's feet.

It took me a long time and I don't know how many experimental casts before I found two methods which would yield a fish from the first third of this attractive pool. The first is to cast at least 70 feet straight down the line of the cliff face from the shallow shelf at the head of the pool. Then, holding the rod as high as possible above the head, one can safely keep the near part of the line from being caught in the swirl of the current. By quickly releasing a further 20 feet of reserve line, you can then make a slow retrieve which quite often results in a strike.

The second method, and a highly unorthodox one, is to enter the pool below the downstream limit of the swirl and to cast upstream at a 45-degree angle. I'm still not sure what happens to the line down in the blue depths of the swirling current, but at least as it swings through there is no sensation of slack line and it is possible to obtain a solid retrieve of the fly close to, or on the bottom. I have heard many anglers say that the headwaters of the Sand just don't hold fish, but on a memorable day in August of 1971 Peter Walters from Oregon and I took eleven fish from this pool before midday, and I didn't move below the swirling water for my five. Try it sometime and see how it produces for you.

Certainly the lower two thirds of the Sand Pool are easier fishing and generally give up more trout. If the river isn't running too high, it is an easy and short wade out to the sandbar in the middle of the pool and from there the lower waters are easily reached with only an average cast. Cast short to begin with, almost straight across stream, allowing the line to swing naturally. When increasing the length of the throw, you will find you have to angle the cast a little more downstream. To compensate for the shallower swing, quickly release 10 or 20 feet of additional line, and let the fly move naturally on the current completely across the tail of the pool. Should the Sand not have been fished before your arrival, the fish will be well distributed throughout the pool, but I have noticed that once the first fish has been hooked and the inevitable commotion has followed, the deep water under the far bank plays host to the trout for the rest of the day.

All things considered, it is a pleasant pool to work, wading is good, and should the fishing be indifferent, there are few stretches of the Tongariro as delightful. After all, where else in the world can one, by only a little patience, have a fantail land on one's rod and, with his eye alert and enquiring, inspect this exciting intruder to his domain? Such is the quiet and peace which prevails on the upper river.

The Blue

The lovely Blue Pool will hold four rods quite comfortably and is one which will allow all to fish in carpet slippers if they so wish. Relatively deep water flows under one's feet practically throughout the length of the pool and the numerous large stones and boulders near the edge make excellent casting platforms. Here is one pool where the expert exponent of long casts will receive his first reward for, especially in the downstream half, the river is wide and relatively slow moving. Certainly, the lower half of the pool is by far the more productive and can yield large bags of good fish, given the right conditions. Casting is relatively easy with only the background of lupins to catch an unwary backcast.

Having once again started with a few short casts in the hope of attracting a fish lying in close, the object should be to try and land the fly as close as possible to the far bank immediately opposite. The pool is comparatively slow-moving and the resulting swing throughout the lie takes a considerable time to reach the near shore once again. Of a consequence one always has the feeling in the Blue that every stone and eddy on the bottom is being explored by the returning fly. It is, I feel, more rewarding to the shooting-head exponent than to the caster of a standard weight-forward line, possibly because of the ease of long casting and the ability of the angler to keep a downstream belly out of the line by keeping the rod tip high throughout the swing.

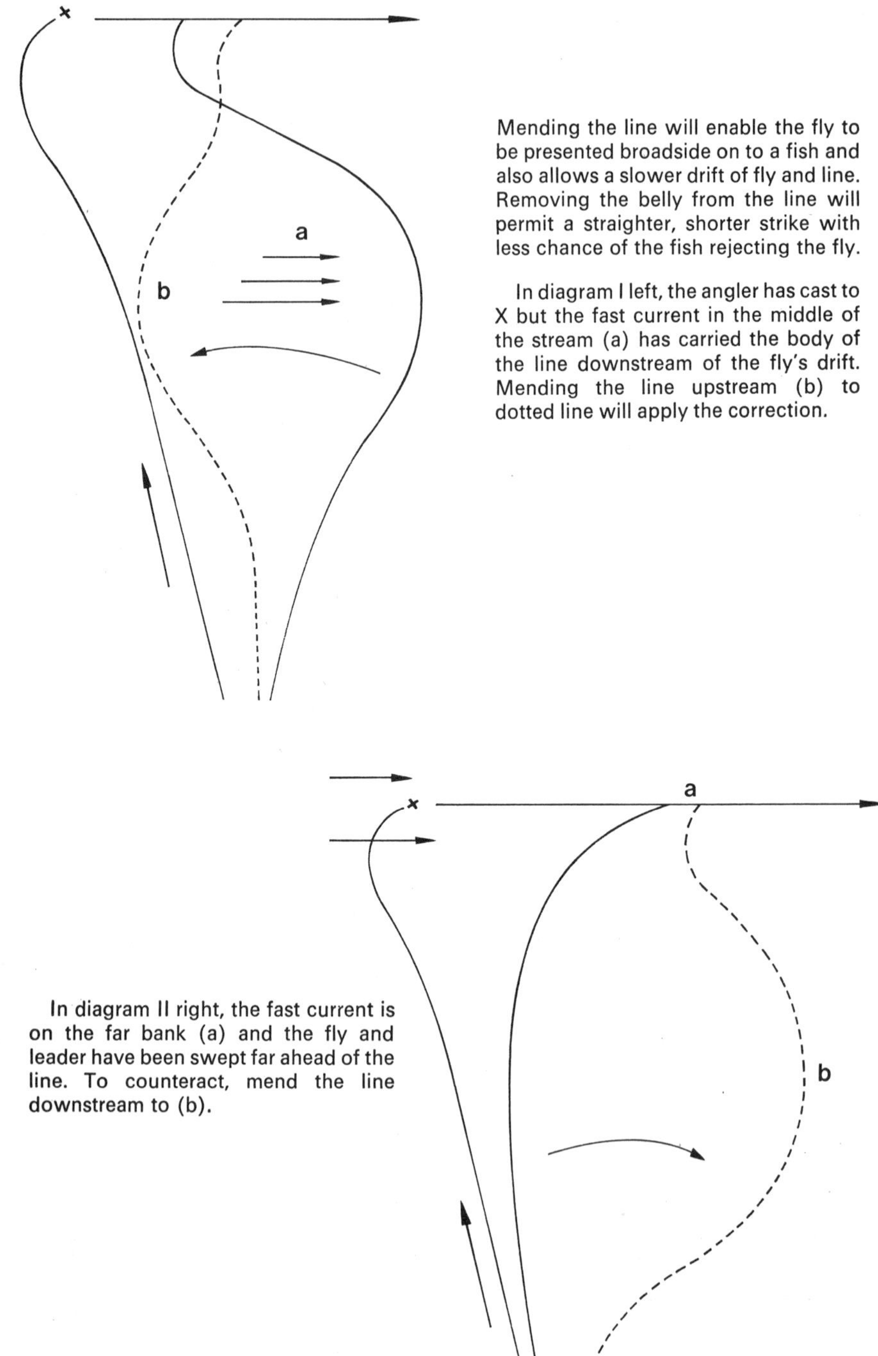

Mending the line will enable the fly to be presented broadside on to a fish and also allows a slower drift of fly and line. Removing the belly from the line will permit a straighter, shorter strike with less chance of the fish rejecting the fly.

In diagram I left, the angler has cast to X but the fast current in the middle of the stream (a) has carried the body of the line downstream of the fly's drift. Mending the line upstream (b) to dotted line will apply the correction.

In diagram II right, the fast current is on the far bank (a) and the fly and leader have been swept far ahead of the line. To counteract, mend the line downstream to (b).

Many fishermen who complain that they have had four or five strikes in a morning and have returned empty-handed for lunch make this basic error: in a pool where the current is faster in the middle than at either side, it is axiomatic that the line will be dragged downstream into a horizontal "U" shape. As a result the touch of the fish is felt only faintly and the strike, unless extremely long and quite brutal, is insufficient to set the hook. The trout has mouthed the fly, decided it is inedible and spat it out to live another day.

A combination of a high rod to keep the maximum amount of line from being pulled downstream by the water pressure, and mending the line by an occasional flip of the rod tip upstream will ensure a straight line from rod to fly. Following the touch of a fish, the strike is then only a question of lifting the rod tip, and the straight pull on the line will set the hook deep and well. We shall still not hook every fish which attacks the fly, but by ensuring a straight line from rod to leader, the percentage of well hooked fish will be far greater.

The Blue is a delightful place to fish but if you have a beginner in tow I feel that there are other pools which may well prove more productive for him. Rarely do casts of less than 60 feet pick up strikes in the Blue, and toward the tail of the pool, 90 to 100 feet is a decided advantage. Anyone for tennis?

CHAPTER 5

THE CLIFF AND THE FAN

THE NEXT MAJOR POOL downstream of the Blue is the Fan, but whereas the Fence, the Sand and the Blue were all fished from the left bank the only satisfactory way to cover all the water here is from the right.

Parking the car at the new Red Hut swingbridge a couple of miles south of Turangi on Highway I, one is then faced with a walk of half an hour at fairly brisk pace to reach firstly, the Cliff and, half a mile further on, the Fan.

The swingbridge itself has encouraged more anglers to make the effort of fishing these pools. Originally carried away in the flood of 1958, it was later replaced by a cagelike contraption strung on a wire hawser 40 feet above the rushing Tongariro. Manpower applied to two ropes—one for going, one for returning—was the means of propulsion and, especially after rain when the manila ropes had become taut, mighty indeed was the effort necessary to gain the opposite bank.

My wife Jo and I had one of our more gruelling experiences of the "flying fox", as these contraptions are known, when making a film for the *American Sportsman* programme for ABC/TV.

The crew consisted of a director, a producer, three cameramen and a sound man. Added to these were the ex rock-and-roll idol of the bobbysox brigade, Fabian, his father-in-law who acted as his manager and, acquired by one of the members of the party, a statuesque blonde ski-instructress, who did little but added much to the general scenery. Jo, Rex Forrester and Ken Wedding from the New Zealand Government Tourist Bureau acted as porters, messengers and general dogsbodies, whilst I was to fish with Fabian and, supposedly, to ensure the success of the venture by catching innumerable fish of acrobatic and aerobatic disposition.

Eventually the film was shown to its United States audience, but the obstacles which had to be overcome were, in turn, numerous, comical, expensive and painful.

The party arrived on a day in September which threatened rain, but the Meteorological Office had either miscalculated or were having their office party when they promised fair to fine weather for the morrow. That night whilst we were becoming acquainted in the hotel over a convivial drink and laying our plan of attack, the heavens opened and forgot to close. Two inches of rain were recorded overnight and by first light the Tongariro was swollen, muddy, unfishable and far from photogenic. General gloom enveloped the group with the exception of the father-in-law-cum-manager of the Star, who moved purposefully and at no mean speed towards the bar. (Perhaps it should be recorded that the same gentleman had the advantage of an expense account from ABC which he was determined to exploit to maximum effect. Only two days later, and after much happiness it was revoked by the producer, who was acting as treasurer for the Company: after all, they were to spend a week in the area, and Pa-in-law seemed to be merely warming to his work.)

It was while we were discussing prospects of the river clearing and the cloudbank lifting that I had my first real shock. Casually, but with interest, I asked Fabian where he had done his fishing back home. With a house in Beverley Hills, Hollywood, I wondered if he had planted fingerlings in his swimming pool in the backyard 10 acres, or whether he jetted the length of the country to Montana for the weekend. "Oh," he said, "I've never fished for trout."

I like to think that I took this bombshell stoically; but Jo, who was beside me, stated afterwards that my eyes glazed, my normally ruddy complexion paled noticeably and that my jaw dropped at least two inches. Her imitation would have been unflattering to a 100 per cent moron.

"You haven't fished for trout?" I squeaked. "Not at all? Never? You mean, surely, that you haven't been out in the past year?".

"No," said our Star, "not ever, but I've trolled for marlin."

Shaken, shattered, I gazed imploringly at the barman who, understanding fellow, gently lifted the glass from my frozen hand and as gently replaced it, replenished.

Slowly, the realisation of what was in store for me came flooding in. Not only did Fabian have to catch fish, but within 24 hours it had to be made to appear to 20 million critical television viewers that he was handling a rod and the fish with expertise. I recalled the old adage that the unachievable will be done immediately but the impossible will take a little longer. This situation definitely belonged in the latter category, and before Fabian had had time to finish his champagne cocktail he was wrapped in a parka and was standing in the drizzle of the dying day on the hotel lawn, rod in hand.

We persevered until dark that evening and Fabian, pleasant fellow that he was, pulled out all the stops and endeavoured to memorise and put to practical use the art of casting a line. By the cessation of hostilities he was showing signs, but still was not going to look convincing on camera. It was resolved by the director, therefore, that whereas we should both fish on the following day, weather permitting, Fabian would continue to practise, and in the event of my hooking a fish it would then be transferred to him as soon as possible. The cameras would then start rolling and to all intents and purposes it would appear that he had hooked it himself. We parted for the night, and a long night it was as everyone tossed and turned wondering what the following day would bring.

It was fine. Spirits revived, and a note of cautious optimism could be detected. The Red Hut Pool and especially the Flying Fox had intrigued the director and it was here that we were to make our first sortie.

Underneath our sweaters we were wired for sound, and told an approximation of what conversation was required of us on the way over the river, and I began the haul across. The ropes were as tightly stretched as guitar strings and the Fox, despite my anxiety for a quick and trouble-free crossing, was as obstinate to budge as a mule.

"I think—*puff*—we'll put you in at the—*pant*—head of the Red Hut—*gasp*—Pool, Fabian," I gulped, trying to follow our "natural" conversation as directed.

"That looks a good bit of water, Tony," said the Star, holding two rods and a smile nicely directed at Camera Three. "Come on back, you guys," hollered the director, "our sound man is having a bit of a problem over here."

Changing ropes and hauling the devil's invention towards the original bank backwards left me speechless, which was probably just as well.

Ten seconds later Lester had his machine in working order and we were off again. I was not to be caught short of breath a second time. "IthinkIwillputyouinattheheadoftheRedHutPoolFabian" I gabbled,

Anglers working the Red Hut Pool.

and waited for his rejoinder. He looked at Camera Three with a nice, open boyish smile and then said "B——! I've forgotten what I was supposed to reply." A yell from the director, a squawk from the sound man, who would have some editing to do that night, and back we went to start all over again.

On the following take (Scene I, Take 3, Cameras, Action,) one of the camera crew complained because we had our heads down while conversing.

Scene I, Take 12, Cameras, Action, finally saw us safely on the far side, our unforgettable discussion recorded for posterity and the guide in a state of collapse and ready to condemn the cage to the depths of the river.

Fabian and I were told to start fishing in the still murky waters of the pool, and had only just got started when a cry came from the other side of the river. We both looked up but could see nothing. In a few minutes the Fox crossed the river with the director being towed over by two cameramen. A few moments later and I heard the worst.

Jo, who had been loading equipment into the cage, had had two fingers crushed between the wire rope and the big riding wheel when the fellows on the far side had begun to pull prematurely. Somehow Ken Wedding had managed to lean back and release her before her fingers were amputated. It must have been a superhuman effort, I realised later. I don't recall what I did with my rod, nor the mad

"You mean to say they won't take a size 16 Black Gnat down here in New Zealand?"

dash to the doctor's surgery in Turangi, but I do remember thinking of Jo's love of her piano and, to a lesser extent, her ability as a typist.

The little finger was a mangled mess, its partner little better. To her everlasting credit and against my expressed bidding she was back on the job in a couple of hours. Twelve stitches in one finger and six in the other couldn't keep her away, and the doctor's confidence in the chances of her fingers' recovery gave her heart. (In the event, she once again plays the piano and assists the family income with her typing. But it was a close thing.)

Back at the river, Fabian had been casting with vigour if not with noticeable success, and I joined him in an effort to bring the first trout into camera lens. The water still looked like milk chocolate and my confidence was at a low ebb. I chose an enormous Turkey and Red tied on a 1/0 hook and opened for business. That fly was so heavy it was like casting its long-departed parent bird and it hit the water like a rock.

An hour of this and I was preparing to change to something more orthodox or, better still, suggest an adjournment to the local, when I felt a strike.

I raised the rod tip once and, because we were using heavy leaders in the discoloured water, gave him another for good measure. There was a minor eruption of water far out in the pool and I was yelling, "Fabian, come and play him." By the time we had met, exchanged rods, got tangled up, freed ourselves, let the fish have slack line, and generally done everything but fall in, my nerves and, I suspect, everyone else's, were visibly pulsing on the surface. Somehow the rod was still bowed and the fish still attached, though quietly sulking on the bottom. The director went through his Scene, Take, Cameras, Action, bit once more, I stumbled off-camera with orders to shout encouragement and appear in time to beach the fish, and we were ready.

Fabian leaned back, pumped the rod once in approved marlin-fighting technique, and looked surprised when the rod stayed upright, unbowed, quite fishless. Had the leader not broken, a rainbow would have landed in the bushes 20 yards behind us. Despite my urgent instructions of the night before to let the fish have line when it wants it, his nerves too, must have slipped far out of neutral.

We held a wake that night, I remember, for in spite of our earnest endeavours until the light failed, not another fish could we coax from that muddy pool that day.

My first thought upon awakening the following morning was a prayer of thanks that I shouldn't have to propel the Flying Fox across-river umpteen more times. The second thought was that the day had dawned clear, and the third that the Tongariro ought to have cleared considerably, and that the fresh should have encouraged a run of fish.

I was right on two counts only: the day remained cloudless and ideal for photography, and there must have been an army of fish in the Red Hut.

American television companies however, leave no stone unturned in obtaining unusual camera angles. Still intrigued by the Flying Fox, our director had hired a light aircraft to convey Harmon aloft, whence he was to film us making our crossing.

Sitting stationary and suspended high above the Tongariro while a stunt pilot manoeuvres his wingtips inches away from tree-covered banks is nerve-wracking. When he passes within feet of one's head in the process it is downright terrifying. For an hour Fabian and I endured the experience all the while reciting our carefully prepared patter. So far as I was concerned, Richard Burton and Sir Laurence Olivier could sleep quiet in their beds. I was no threat to their image.

Our composure returned after lunch and, for me at any rate, the serious business of the day began. In fewer than half a dozen casts I had a fish hit hard and the tricky business of exchanging rods began again. Thirty seconds later the fish was on its way rejoicing, but still wondering how it was to remove the Mrs Simpson from its jaw. I tied on another Mrs S. Ten minutes later and I had another. It took hold so hard I felt as if someone had dropped a boulder on to my rod tip. It broached then, far out in the eye of the current, red stripe showing, big, strong, angry, male. We changed rods. The director intoned his litany of Scene, Take etc., etc., the cameramen expressed their readiness. The soundman nodded his satisfaction. The producer smiled his approval. Father-in-law poured another double-header. The Big Blonde proceeded with her manicure. Jo, Rex and Ken prayed. I bounced into camera view chanting, "Stick to him, Fab, you've got a beauty there."

Fabian looked puzzled: "But I haven't," he said, "the bloody thing got off a few seconds ago."

It is next to impossible to lose six consecutive fish, but we managed to do so during that afternoon. Sometimes they made good their escape during the rod exchange, more often after a couple of leaps, and no. 6 had the audacity to fall off the hook when only a couple of feet from shore. I tried to grab the latter in approved cowboy bull-dogging style, and got only wet arms and a feeling of abject foolishness for my trouble.

Light was becoming a problem for the camera crew when I tied into the seventh. It had been resolved, in desperation, that I should play it until it was virtually drowned before passing the rod to Fabian. Never have I worked a fish so carefully. Whenever he wanted an inch, I let him have it. If he jumped I dropped my rod tip. If he sulked I let him sulk.

Gradually I eased him towards the shore, nursed him through the flurry of panic when he felt the shallows under his belly, and called for my partner to land him. Fabian stepped forward, the exchange was completed. I stepped back—and fell ignominiously over a rock into 18 inches of icy water.

Dripping, I staggered erect. The tanned young hero had successfully beached a beautiful 7-pound male and was holding it up in approved style before three madly whirring cameras.

Harmon, chief of the camera crew spoke softly: "I don't think we've had enough light for the past five minutes."

Grown men in tears is a pitiful sight.

Later in the week we were to get some good action which I shall recount later.

Losing the fish was bad enough, but the thing which really hurt me to the quick was the time and energy we expended on the Flying Fox. I have seen the film, and the time devoted to our method of transportation was exactly 6 seconds of viewing. Aircraft hire, near-coronary for the guide, near-amputations for Jo—and all for six seconds!

Three years ago the Fox was again replaced by a swingbridge, but to many of us it is a mixed blessing. Whereas many fishermen either did not wish to expend the effort of the crossing, or were unashamedly terrified of it, the exertion necessary to traverse the Tongariro nowadays is comparable to wandering down to the letter-box. Consequently the Red Hut, and indeed most pools which require casting from the right bank become, in the flush of the season, a veritable forest of rods.

The Cliff

To reach the Fan and the Cliff pools, turn right over the swing-bridge and follow a well defined track upstream, keeping the By-Pass, a breakaway of the Tongariro, on your right. Twenty minutes of steady walking will bring you to the Cliff, a small pool of infinite charm. Pines crest the sheer bank on the far side and a sandy beach provides an ideal recreation spot for the children if they have accompanied you.

A word of warning here: as you approach the head of the pool to begin your fishing, stay well back from the water's edge. The fish, if undisturbed by prior activity, are inclined to be in quite close, and I have counted 30 with no more than 18 inches of water above them, basking in the sun. You will, naturally, be able to take only one before they move off into deeper cover, but we have all known the day when one is better than none.

The Cliff is an easy pool to work. A few short casts into the head of the pool, and, increasing line, aim about 30 degrees down stream.

It is not particularly deep from about the halfway mark, and to avoid a few large boulders in the middle, I usually cast more downstream and across the further I move. In other words, fish shallower than you would normally do. It is inclined to be less expensive on tackle and will still produce strikes.

Incidentally, the Cliff is fishable from both sides, but I find I have more success from the right bank.

The Fan

Upstream, perhaps half a mile beyond the Cliff, is the Fan Pool. Having located the path at the head of the Cliff and forced your way through lupins which climb far above your head, it is only a question of following the riverbank to the glassy water which always indicates the depth of a resting area for the trout.

The pool is aptly named, for the water rushes white from the Big Bend above and forces its way through a narrow entrance into the head of the Fan. For the first 20 yards, it swirls, with back eddies and currents taking control of one's line, and I have had little luck in this section.

Once the river has decided to continue on its interrupted way, however, there are perhaps 80 yards of water which can and do produce trout. A few large boulders excepted, it is fairly comfortable wading until one nears the tail of the pool, where the current accelerates and the rocks, though smaller, are treacherously round and slippery. You won't drown if you slip, but it's a long cold walk back to the car on a breezy day in July.

For the most part, the trout seem to lie under the far bank. I base this upon two assumptions. First, the strike almost always seems to come before the fly has swung back to a line immediately below the angler. In other words, the fish has evinced interest in it quite soon after it has hit the water, and has followed it around to make the touch early in its path.

Secondly—and here is something for you to try on a day when the pools are overstocked with rods and not with fish—I was witness to an amazing demonstration when fishing the Fan Pool in August of last year.

I had taken two fish by 11 o'clock in the morning after arriving at the pool just before 10. Well satisfied, I had stopped for a cup of coffee, and in a mood of contentment known only to the angler who has enjoyed good sport and has a reach of river to himself without competition, was daydreaming luxuriously. Quite suddenly the fairly dense brush on the opposite side of the pool parted, a head appeared, disappeared, and again came into view 10 yards upstream, preceded by a rod.

"This'll be funny," I thought. "If he doesn't fall in he'll be lucky, and if he tries to cast he'll be birdnesting all day."

He didn't do either, but he hooked five good fish in the next hour and a half while I, from the "correct" side of the river had to be content with one more, and that an ugly, black jack whose head weighed more than the rest of him.

My unknown friend landed only two of his five, for he couldn't follow the fish downstream and had the devil of a time bringing them up to him. He had, however, had the foresight to bring a net, rarely seen on the river, and managed to coax these two over it. The method was simplicity itself. He merely let 30 yards or so of line go downstream on the current, communed with nature for a while, and then slowly wound it back on his reel.

I haven't had a chance in the last few months to try the pool from that side, but on my next trip up to the Blue or Sand pools, I'm making a detour in the direction of the Fan. What's more, I'm including some really heavy monofilament in my tackle, and for the first time in years I'll be carrying a collapsible landing net up the Tongariro.

Perhaps it was a fluke, but it certainly verified my guess that most of the trout in the Fan lie under the protection of the overhanging trees and scrub.

Whatever your luck up at the Cliff and the Fan, it's a pleasant walk, and you are less likely to meet competition up there than you are in some of the more accessible pools. And with the growth in the popularity of angling as a sport, that's a pretty important consideration these days.

CHAPTER 6

THE POUTU

WHERE THE POUTU RIVER, the natural outlet of Lake Rotoaira, joins the Tongariro the waters meet suspiciously, swirling, touching, withdrawing, finally accepting each other and gliding serenely into one of the loveliest pools of the river. It was from this Poutu Pool that I was afforded one of my more embarrassing fishy experiences. It is only now, in retrospect, that I can find amusement in a ridiculous situation.

A world conference of surgeons was held last year in Melbourne, and it was from this city that I received a telephone call one evening, asking if I'd be free to act as guide to an American doctor for two days of the following week.

Over an indifferent connection the client sounded gruff, impatient, and not a little demanding, but business had been quiet for a week or so and I gladly accepted the reservation. It was only as we were finishing the conversation that he produced his crunch line. "You guided a colleague of mine last year on the Tongariro. He caught a rainbow of 7¾ pounds which he had mounted. *I want a bigger one*." Not you will note, "I'd love to beat it", or "It'd be fun to head him off", or even "Hope I can do as well." Just "I want a bigger one!"

I started to explain that 8-pounders couldn't always be produced to order, especially in the middle of February, but the operator interrupted with some nonsense about "Three minutes and did he wish to extend . . . " and he hung up. I returned to the television set in thoughtful mood. Jo, attempting to soothe, reminded me that only a few days before I had taken two fish in excess of 8 pounds each from the Red Hut Pool. My reaction, of course, was that the law of averages was even more against success because of this, and I retired to bed with a nagging worry based somewhere in the pit of my stomach.

The good doctor eventually arrived and my worst fears were confirmed.

"Hi, Tony," he said. "Got that big one all staked out for me?"

Now this question is generally par for the course from visiting anglers, but this fellow really meant it.

"Well . . ." I said.

"Fine, fine," he interrupted. "Let's go get him bright and early in the morning. Five o'clock OK with you?"

I said that five o'clock was certainly OK with me, but I couldn't guarantee . . .

"See you then, young fellow, I'm for bed if we've an early start. Good night."

I found myself outside the hotel wondering if one of the other guides would be available to take over my booking.

"Courage," said a small voice. "Think of your starving wife and cocker spaniel. Think of your bank manager's forced smile. Contemplate the approaching winter with a tent for accommodation." My chin went up, a light of resolve came into my eyes and I started to think positively. Dale Carnegie lasted five seconds flat.

My dreams that night were centred around hundreds of fish caught by my doctor on the following day. All measured exactly 13½ inches and had to be returned to the water. With each one his rage became more awful. With each one I died a thousand deaths.

The day dawned magnificently. Cloudless, windless, the promise of heat already evident, the river eminently fishable. A day in which one would usually rejoice.

My prayers of the previous night had not been answered. No flash flood had transformed the Tongariro into a raging murky torrent. No 90-knot wind had materialised. No urgent cable had recalled the doctor to an ailing benefactor of his hospital. "Somebody up there," I decided, "doesn't like me."

Indeed, the doctor himself looked disgustingly healthy. Resplendent in scarlet—jacket, trousers, hat, even socks were scarlet—he greeted me at the hotel entrance.

"Let's go get him, Tony," he said. "I'm feeling kinda lucky today, and my friend says you know every fish in the river on a first-name basis."

I tried to play it smart. "Sure," I told him, "but I'm worried about Harriet and Herbert. They're normally in the Red Hut Pool on the 8th of February and they hadn't arrived yesterday. They should be around twelve pounds this year."

"That's the ticket," said the doctor. "Think big. Just as long as I can get one bigger than that one Joe got last year, you and I will get along fine."

"That," I thought, "was a beautiful but rather short friendship."

We drove to the Red Hut Bridge, and while my client donned his new Hodgman waders, I reconnoitred the pool. There was only one angler fishing. "Good," I thought. "At least the competition for the monster won't be too fierce."

Doctor joined me, new rod, reel and line fairly sparkling in the early morning sun, every step exuding limitless confidence in my ability to provide a fish worthy of the equipment and his not unimpressive dignity.

"Where do we start, boy?"

What with "young fellow" and "boy" I was beginning to wonder if he regarded anyone who was not drawing National Superannuation as positively juvenile. I indicated the pool below the bridge.

"Can't go there," he said. "Someone's fishing it."

Gently, I tried to explain that I had seen a dozen rods in that pool in the height of the spawning run, and that all had been bent at some time during the day. Reluctantly he agreed to "give it a whirl for a few minutes".

I eased him out over the big boulders at the head, treacherous as iced glass with a summer accumulation of weed, and instructed him to cast straight across river. It was then that I asked if he were left-handed, for the handle of the reel was assuredly on the southpaw side of the rod. He denied it. Thinking that he might perhaps use the method employed by spin-casters, casting righthanded and retrieving left, I made further enquiry. He didn't do that either. "Mightn't it then be better to reverse the reel?" I enquired. He thought it a good idea.

Nagging doubts were assailing my mind with each passing second. My memories of his friend and colleague were vivid. He had arrived in late May, had fished long and tirelessly for a week, had taken to the Tongariro as if it had flowed at his back door since boyhood, and had cast a disciplined if not spectacular line. He had, moreover, been blessed with an almost continuous run of good fish. He most certainly had not mounted his reel back to front.

Having remedied the situation, Doctor was ready to begin. Gingerly, he pulled 6 feet of line from the reel and began to cast and cast and cast and cast . . . No sooner had the fly hit the water than it was whisked up into the air once more. Down, up, down, up—6 feet of line and 8 feet of leader. Down, up, down, up.

Quietly, I suggested to him that were a suicidal trout to move with the speed of light, it would still be denied the opportunity to realise on its death-wish.

"Just getting the feel of it," he said. "New rod, you know."

Suspicion had now darkened into certainty. I wanted, nay, needed to cry. My doctor who had ordered, demanded, insisted upon a fish that even the perennial angler would cherish, had never fly-fished before in his life. From afar he had seen someone, sometime, going through the motions.

You waved a rod and you caught a trout. As simple as that.

"Peel off a few more yards and cast that too," I suggested, none too hopefully. The result was chaos. Line was encircled around my client's neck, the fly bobbed sick and dying at his feet.

By virtue of necessity I am a kindly soul. All too often have I had the task of enticing a fish on to a beginner's line, and the unconcealed delight on the countenance of the tyro when he holds up his first trophy, is a satisfying reward. But at least they all admit they are novices. Not once throughout the two days did my distinguished surgeon admit he had never fished for trout with a fly rod. Renowned, masterful, in complete control of any situation, he might have been—as a surgeon; as a fly caster his timing was non-existent, his impatience quite extraordinary, his temper volatile, and his fingers as nimble as ten thumbs.

We persevered. I demonstrated. I coaxed. I flattered. I damn near despaired. The man quite simply would not listen.

To add to the joys, our downstream neighbour was landing his second fish. I needed a change of company, so excused myself for a moment and went to witness the *coup-de-grace*. Something which could have been a .22 bullet hit me a resounding blow on the jaw. For some reason best known to himself my client had commenced to cast directly upstream at the time I was passing behind him.

Something akin to hatred flooded through me as I gingerly removed a size 6 Mallard and Yellow from my offended face. I counted to ten quite slowly, and because there seemed little change, did so again.

Handing him back his fly, I proceeded on my mission. There had been no apology; merely a testy look which said plainly, "That cast would have taken a fish if you hadn't got your big ugly face in the way."

"Having a rough time of it?" asked a friendly American voice.

He had landed his trout, a beautiful hen of about 6 pounds, and was gently releasing her back into the river.

"Not really," I said, catching pints of blood in my handkerchief, "You strike one of these every season, and I'm getting mine over early this year."

"I've been listening to you both," he told me. "The bastard makes me ashamed that I come from the same Continent."

"He wants nothing under eight pounds," I said. His eyes popped out as if they were on crutches.

"Eight pounds! That baby I just released might have gone six, and that's the biggest I've taken in either the North or South Islands. I've been here a month," he added helpfully.

That did it. I charged my way back into the Red Hut, took my client firmly by the arm and said "You'll not catch a fish here if you stay till Doomsday. You don't cast far enough. We're going up to the Poutu Pool and there you're going to do as I damned well tell you."

He didn't like it, but he came. His massive dignity had been affronted, but he came. Nobody, I am sure, had spoken to him like that since he had been caught asleep in lecture at medical school.

The Poutu is made for casters of the calibre of my client. It helps, of course, if one can hit the far bank and have the fly move slowly throughout the width of the pool, but providing one manages to feed off the line down the current on the right bank, there is often a fishy dunce in the school prepared to have a snap. Surely, it's railing, and railing is frowned upon by the proponents of a piscatorial equivalent of Hoyle, but desperation brooks no barrier.

At a near canter, I led my doctor upstream on the well-trodden path created by a thousand hopeful anglers. Three hundred yards onward the track forks; to the left it meanders up to the Cliff and Fan pools, straight ahead and down into a fern-laced glen lies the way to the Poutu. Gentle ponga ferns form soft green parasols overhead and the air is cool.

"What a delightful spot," he puffed, and my anger abated a notch or two. Anyone who can appreciate an unspoiled example of nature's native handiwork couldn't be *all* bad.

We forded the By-Pass and moved up the old, dried-up riverbed to our new water.

"It's pretty," he said, gazing at the pool, and my ire abated a little more.

There is a sandbar at the head of the pool and I led him out on to it.

"Get some line out, any old way," I told him. "Then feed out about twenty-five yards straight down the current, count to ten slowly, and then retrieve it."

He went through his up, down, up, down routine a couple of dozen times, let the fly settle and began to follow instructions.

As with people, there must be fish with an overdeveloped sense of curiosity. Instead of cowering under the far bank at the commotion, as I had no doubt her every schoolmate had done, a halfwitted hen felt compelled to investigate.

Perhaps the sight of a Mallard and Yellow swimming backwards proved too enticing to resist. Perhaps she became entangled in the coils of line preceding the fly, and in an endeavour to free herself became hooked in the mouth, perhaps she was not merely halfwitted. We shall never know.

There was a startled exclamation from the medical profession, a sudden bow in the new rod, an agitated flapping almost at our feet and an incredulous, spontaneous cry of disbelief from the guide. He had hooked a fish, or was it vice versa?

My shouted instructions seemed only to confuse him into performing their reverse. He gave line when he should have retrieved. He entered into a massive tug-of-war when he should have been as gentle as a mother with her infant. "Look at her jump" he screamed. Jump? She has just been hoisted bodily from the water.

If ever a fish deserved to be lost, this was it. After three minutes her spirit was broken. She died, not of asphyxia through drowning, but of a massive heart attack after a severe manhandling. I can still see the look of reproach in her eye. Doctor was, at first, jubilant. He chuckled, he chortled, he crowed. "Not bad eh, Tony?" he asked. "Reckon I handled that baby real good. There was just no way she was going to get away."

"No way," I thought, "except by breaking off, or having the rod smash or tearing the fish's head off its shoulders. The Lord knows what would have happened if it had been the 8-pounder he wants."

The next question was inevitable. "What do you reckon it weighs, boy?" I looked at the still quivering form, had a mental guess, added two pounds as an undeserved bonus, and blurted out, "Six pounds."

His face fell and it was obvious that my answer had failed to please.

"Is that all?" he asked. "Well, that's no good to me at all, is it?"

"It's in beautiful condition," I said, in a vain attempt to cheer him. "It'll make a splendid dinner tonight."

He was not consoled. "Don't eat them," he said.

He sulked throughout the remainder of the day and, try as we might, no other trout was idiot enough to make the mistake of accepting our poorly presented offering. It was a silent drive back to the hotel.

"Same time in the morning?" I enquired, hoping against hope that he had decided to try his luck in Iceland or Peru.

"S'pose so," he said. "G'night."

To confess that the evening was spent in trying to conjure up an excuse for absenteeism the following day, would be to state the obvious. Never, before or since, have I longed so desperately for a cancellation of a succeeding day's activities.

Once again a morning of unparalleled beauty greeted us. A hint of gold in the eastern sky slowly penetrated the early haze and the murmur of the river was the only sound to disturb the silence. Apart from a gruff "Morning", I had received no other greeting. I tried a confident whistled tune, but even to my ears it resembled a dirge. I let the silence envelop us.

Now the Red Hut is not the only pool on the Tongariro to hold fish in February, but with the river at low level it has the advantage of depth over many of the others, and fish like depth if they can find it. It is always a good holding pool, and with summer flow it is, possibly, the easiest place to take a trout.

I peered over the bank and was appalled to see four men working it industriously. Further, they could all cast a country mile, I noted, and would make my client look as competent as a mannequin in a football scrum.

"Bit crowded this morning," I muttered. "Let's go and have a look at Major Jones."

Major Jones was playing host to five anglers.

"You got one out of the Poutu yesterday," I reminded him. "Perhaps its grandmother has arrived by now."

It was becoming a bit of a one-sided conversation and I know my voice was taking on a desperate edge. A quick look upstream from the Red Hut bridge assured us that the pool was ours, and a quarter of an hour saw us once more on the sandbar.

It was now after 6 o'clock, and although the sun was steadily climbing, I selected a Mrs Simpson, Red Body size 6, for my doctor. It is a favourite early-morning fly of mine, and before wetting it, I murmured a benediction over it. Doctor went through his tortuous motions, I looked on helplessly, Mrs Simpson hit the placid waters of the pool like a golfball, and our long day had begun.

At 8 o'clock we had coffee and changed to a Red Setter. At 10 we had coffee and a Mallard and Yellow. At noon we returned to the hotel, where he lunched. At 2 we tied on a Leslie's Lure. At 4 I had used every fly in my box.

To be fair, he did show stamina. His willpower was astounding, his grim, silent determination revealed a depth of intestinal fortitude rarely encountered. When all is said and done, any man who requires 20 false casts to project a fly to a maximum of 20 feet must have an arm of lead as the day nears its end. He persevered. I knew a helplessness beyond relief and swore to take up embroidery as a profession.

The sun begins to dip over the mountains at about 7 o'clock in February. Shadows lengthened over the pool. Doctor was still casting. Up, down, up, down, *ad infinitum*. Only the car lights on the main highway now relieved the total darkness and my client was only a vague shape at my elbow.

Finally he spoke. "Six more casts and that's it."

"Home," I thought. "Wonderful, peaceful, untroubled home. Here I come."

Something was nagging at my conscience, however. The man had tried so desperately, so long and with such concentration. And I had failed him.

"Let's tie on a Hairy Dog for the last few casts then," I suggested.

Resignedly, he passed me the rod tip for the hundredth time and I made the change. Wearily, he began his casting. Slowly, he started his retrieve. It happened.

Doctor emitted a strangled gasp. There was the unmistakable splash of a panicking fish a few yards below us, the reel began to scream with a sound that to us was the sweetest of orchestrations.

"Let him run," I yelled, and groping, pulled his right hand from the handle of the reel. "Keep your damned rod tip *up*!"

It was a long run, full of purpose, but at no stage after the first smashing strike did the fish rise again. Somewhere out in the darkness of the pool it halted, shaking its head from side to side.

"Carefully, now," I warned. "Don't horse him or you'll break him off."

Knowing my client's reaction of the previous day, I had changed to 9 lb breaking-strain leader without disclosing the fact, but I was still worried. The fish decided that the head of the pool was more to its liking. It came at us with a rush, gaining yards of slack line in the process.

"Forget the reel, reef in line," I hollered.

"What do you mean?" he panicked.

Somehow in the dark I found the line and took in ten yards in as many quick pulls. Our fish, thank God, was still attached.

"Now hold the line in your left hand and try and pick up the slack with the reel," I implored. The fish, bless it, lay doggo while he did.

"Start to move toward the bank," I suggested and immediately wished I hadn't, as he stumbled over a stone. He swore, loudly and profanely, but a swirl almost at my feet reassured me. Another short run, relatively uneventful, and Doctor was high and dry on the bank.

"Where the hell is it?" he begged. "I can't see it at all".

There was an ominous splashing a yard from shore and I brought out my torch. My first glimpse was of a tail. A big, beautiful, wide tail. My next revealed that the leader was wrapped around a boulder just above the fly. I know I swore. I know I panicked. I know I dived at that fish with both arms extended, plunged them into the water behind him and with a lunge heaved him twenty feet up the bank.

He was ours. My torch still glowed under two feet of water where I had dropped it, but he was ours. Scrambling over the boulders, we gazed down at him. In the blackness, his dim shape looked large. I retrieved the torch and we peered again.

Doctor let out a whoop. "It's bigger than Joe's—I know it is."

I took out my scales, determined to lie to any limits to make it bigger than Joe's. There was no need: $8\frac{1}{4}$ lb of male rainbow had succumbed to the blandishments of my novice.

His joy was unconfined. His whole personality was transformed. He hugged me, slapped me on the back, made inarticulate sounds deep in his chest, told me a dozen times how I was "the best goddam guide in the world".

The homeward journey was a joyous interlude. Between bursts of song he insisted Jo and I join him for the "biggest goddam celebration that little ol' hotel had ever known".

Our arrival at the foyer was, to say the least, embarrassing. Two guests who were checking in were startled to have a trout thrust inches from their faces by a wildlooking man in scarlet. "What do you think of that? Isn't it a beauty?" he roared.

Having received the congratulations of the reception staff, he wheeled in the direction of the lounge, where guests sipping coffee looked amazed, aghast or amused as the fish was paraded for all to admire. Onward he sped to the diningroom, demanding praise of the assembled gathering, through the swinging doors of the kitchen, where chefs, pantrymaids and waitresses were all given the opportunity to exclaim over his prize. Excuse myself as I might, I was compelled to act as aide-de-camp to the performance. Embarrassing? Yes. But now, in retrospect, an hilarious half hour.

He was as good as his word. He dined and wined us in lordly fashion. His trophy now adorns the waitingroom at his surgery, so he writes me, and is the subject of much admiration.

Jo informs me however that on occasions my sleep becomes disturbed and I cry out in the night something that sounds like No! No! No! Obviously I have just received a dream telephone call which says, "You guided Doctor— on the Tongariro last year and he caught an 8¼ rainbow which he had mounted. *I want a bigger one*!"

Yes, the Poutu Pool has many memories and is a pleasant spot to spend a few hours. To fish it, ignore the quarter-acre or so of disturbed water where the rivers meet and concentrate on the long glide of the main pool. Fish it relatively shallow by casting 30 degrees downstream, for it currently holds a pair of disagreeable snags, to one of which is attached at least a couple of lines. Should the reader, one day before the next flood removes them permanently, happen to snare a size 10 shooting taper from the lower of these, my address for the return is in the local telephone book. . . .

CHAPTER 7

FROM THE RED HUT TO THE BREAKFAST

TO STATE THAT THE Red Hut Pool is an outstanding holding area for fish is to declare the obvious to anyone who can "read" water. Firstly, it has depth, a factor which trout favour above all others. Further, below the pool, the Tongariro accelerates through rapids for nearly half a mile before reaching the Shag Pool, and it is through this fast and tiring water that the fish must move before the peace of the Red Hut affords them rest. Add to these the relatively slow pace of the river through the pool and the consequent slow drift of the fly through the lies, and you have the perfect example of eminently fishy water.

Unlike many other pools on the river, Red Hut has four distinct "hot spots" where the angler may stand and cast with anticipation and confidence.

Stand on the swingbridge so as to overlook the water near the right bank and, armed with polarised glasses against the glare, you will see sometimes 30 or 40 fish resting in the quiet current supplied by the By-Pass, a breakaway tributary of the Tongariro proper.

To fish to them it is necessary to cross the By-Pass and walk downstream to the sandspit 20 yards upstream of the bridge. I have most success casting to the right bank and fishing at a 45-degree angle downstream, landing the fly as close to the overhanging brush as possible. Immediately the fly touches the water, quickly release a further 10 or 20 feet of reserve line, mending this in against the bank as it is released. The lure will than sink rapidly and hug the bank under which the fish are sheltering. I make the retrieve once again up through the fish by extending the rod tip as close to the bank as I can, and generally bring back the line at a more rapid pace than I use for heavier and faster water.

I know many anglers who state that whereas they might take one

The Red Hut Pool and solitary angler, as seen from the Shag Pool.

fish in this lie they seldom get more, claiming that the commotion caused by the first makes the others wary. Perhaps this is true on occasions, but I have had some wonderful hours in this relatively unfished spot. Probably, a bonny day in September of last year provided the shining example of just how profitable the tail of the By-Pass can be.

The National Film Unit had requested some action shots of leaping fish for their library and I had agreed to try and snare an unwitting trout filmstar. In order to have a second string to my bow I suggested that my friend John Fenwick, a talented and fanatical fisherman from Auckland who was spending a couple of days as our guest, join us. John elected to fish the Red Hut Pool and I was content to try an hour from the sandspit.

It is rarely that things go according to plan when a movie camera is poised and waiting for action, but that morning was unforgettable. By lunch John had taken 5 fish from the big pool and I had landed 6 from the By-Pass exit. Moreover, one could swear that every fish knew it was to have its antics recorded for posterity. They were wild! They jumped feet from the water, they tail-walked almost up to the lens of the camera and jumped again. They thought they were marlin. Our cameraman, Martin Barriball, was kept at the run throughout the morning, but was a happy though exhausted man as we sat down to our sandwiches at midday.

For my part, I had but one regret. Martin had suggested I be available for three days in case the fishing was difficult, but within three hours he had more film to develop than he could possibly use. I had successfully angled my way out of a retainer for the remaining 20 hours. I have, however, warned him that next time I shall make certain that the hook I use is barbed. After all, though I love to fish, I also enjoy eating, and one's job must precede pleasure in importance.

In order to fish the head of the Red Hut it is necessary to be a sure-footed and strong wader. The boulders are numerous, large, round and slippery, and the current from the By-Pass stronger than it looks. I don't often use a wading-stick, but if the river is running even a little higher than usual, this is one crossing where I favour a third leg.

At the confluence of the main stream and the By-Pass there is a quiet backwater, almost on the edge of the drop into the pool, and it is here you will take up station. Fishing is simplicity itself and casting of little importance. The current downstream is strong and will carry line and fly as far as you wish it to go. Without exception the trout will take on the retrieve, if they are so inclined, and then begins the task of staying upright while playing the fish and wading back to shore through the maze of stones. I've seen more duckings in the head-waters of the Red Hut Pool than in all other reaches of the Tongariro combined. But it will produce fish for the angler who is confident enough to take his courage firmly in hand—and that, after all, is the name of the game.

Three exposed large stones mark the position in the pool which I prefer to all others. A cast straight across river to the far bank and a quick feeding of an additional 20 or 30 feet of line mended upstream to remove the belly from the line, is rewarded with a reassuringly slow, deep swing of the fly through the lie. A strike can result anywhere throughout the path of the swing and with the deep channel almost under one's rod tip, the retrieve is likely to produce action only yards from the angler. Incidentally, the Red Hut is genuine shooting-head country and I'm satisfied that this tackle will provide twice as many strikes as the standard weight-forward line. Don't hesitate to cast a little upstream if the river is running high. The secret of catching trout in the Red Hut is sinking the fly, and the man who fails to achieve this object will be fishing to kill time, not fish.

The tail of the pool can provide excellent sport when the river is losing volume after a flood or fresh. Probably because visibility is better in the shallower water at such times, the fish seem to congregate in this section. Cast a little downstream to avoid the odd snag which is invariably a hazard of the shallows, and do not be in too much haste to begin the retrieve. Many fish are taken close in against the right bank, and are left unmolested if the fly is not permitted to reach them. The lower part of the pool seems to me to fish better in the early morning and late evening rather than during the middle of the day. Presumably, the trout prefer more water over their backs when the sun is high.

I have seen a few anglers trying to fish from the left bank in the Red Hut. Roll-casting is the only means of getting a line out apart from feeding it straight from the reel. I have seen an odd fish accept the offering too, but hours per trout would be comparable to gallons per mile in a motorcar—totally uneconomical.

It was in the Red Hut that I had one of the most drawn-out battles with a fish I can recall. I rose early one morning and surprisingly had the pool to myself. Within ten minutes I was fast into a fish which stayed close to the bottom and was unbelievably heavy. Twenty minutes later I had lost line, and the heaviest trout I had ever hooked in the Tongariro was preparing to tumble out of the pool and into the long rapid below. I gave him the butt, but slowly and surely he gained line and the chase was on. Down through the churning white water he barrelled, whilst I dodged stones and treetrunks in the mad chase after him. As quickly as I gained line he peeled it from the reel again. By now I was guessing at his weight; 10 lb? Nearer 15 lb? A brownie, I decided, and far in excess of the 13½-pounder I had taken earlier in the season from the Poutu Pool. Somehow the leader had not parted at the knot, nor had it snagged one of the numerous exposed rocks which abound in the rapid. Slowly, inevitably, he was being drawn closer to my side of the river and away from the fast current. A cluster of large stones 15 yards from shore gave me the opportunity to head him in that direction and finally, as exhausted as the fish, I was able to draw him into the shallows on the far side of the little island where his flapping assured me he was close to high and dry. Maintaining pressure and retrieving line on to the reel as I waded out, I again guessed at his weight.

A male brown worthy of the record books, I promised myself, and peered over the rocks at my pride and joy: firmly and inescapably hooked through the dorsal fin was a 4 lb rainbow in only average

Sequence of success at the Red Hut Pool.

condition. Despite a rod bent almost double, I had been unable to draw a fish broadside on into the heavy waters of the Red Hut. Try it sometime with a dead fish and you'll appreciate the difficulties you'll encounter with one in full control of its faculties.

Disgustedly, I unhooked him, and perhaps not as gently as is my usual practice, I turned him loose. It had taken nearly 50 minutes to gain control of the situation, and my disappointment was compounded when, upon looking upstream, I found no fewer than four rods had arrived during my temporary absence.

"Did you lose him after all that?" one of them enquired as I made my way back again.

"No", I told him. "I got the fish. It's my morale that's gone."

I enjoy the Red Hut Pool immensely but, as noted elsewhere, it is rarely that it does not play host to many rods, some of whom are reluctant to move through the pool as etiquette demands. Perhaps I am labouring this subject at the risk of a reader's yawn, but angling is a sport, undertaken for enjoyment and relaxation, and no sporting recreation is completely pleasurable if its courtesies are flouted or ignored.

The Shag

The Shag Pool has only of recent months come into its own as a consistent provider of fish. The lower river level has made it possible to wade out for about 10 feet from the right-hand bank, thus enabling a normal cast to be made without the fly hanging up in the overhanging brush at one's back. Take up position with a lone toe-toe bush behind you and, contrary to normal practice, aim your cast upstream and across to the middle of the cliff face opposite. Immediately the fly touches the water, mend line upstream two or three times to remove the belly the fast intervening water will make, elevate the rod as high as you can and be rewarded with a slow, fish-tempting swing of the fly down the lie. As a general rule the strike will be made as the fly is just downstream of your casting position and on the far side of the fast channel. Then comes the fun. The fish in this pool have a lot going for them. At the tail, the river divides. If they take the right-hand bank side, you can follow them through quiet water, but if they choose the alternative escape route they are unlikely to apply the brakes until they reach the Duchess Pool downstream, and there's no way to keep pace with them through all that tumbling white water.

In frustration because of the number of rods in the more productive areas I have, on occasion, taken fish from the left-bank side. By perching on the path cut into the cliff and roll-casting from that position, one can often entice a strike, but I soon tire of having my fly move through the same arc *ad infinitum*, and a quarter hour finds me becoming bored.

The Duchess

Trevor Thompson suggested to me the other day that the Duchess Pool would fish very much more easily if one were able to cut a path along the cliff edge on the right-hand bank. I agree wholeheartedly, for with the sun at the right angle one can see fish lying hard in under the bank from the heights of the cliff above. I have tried every means short of drowning to cast from the sandy shelf, which is wadeable from the head of the pool for 15 yards or so, and obtain a strike from the right bank. To no avail. The trouble appears to be the difficulty in sinking the fly, after a necessary 90- or 100-foot cast, sufficiently rapidly to interest a fish lying in 4 or 5 feet of water. I have tried upstream and across, slightly downstream with the rapid release of 30 feet of reserve line, standard technique, and all have produced the same ignominious result. It is not that I haven't caught fish when casting from the left bank towards the right, but the fish which do attack do so when the fly has swung almost entirely through the width of the river.

In other words, they are trout lying nearer to the left-bank side. Perhaps some kindly soul whose knowledge is greater will confide his secret to me? Meantime, I intend to encourage Trevor's musings to the point of action, even if it means lending a hand with a shovel.

The Duchess yields particularly well following a fresh in the Tongariro. With an abundance of lupins up to 8 feet high on the left bank, normal casting is reduced to quartering downstream, but the fish lie quite close into the bank, and the fly has sunk sufficiently by the time it reaches them. It is a difficult pool to wade with confidence, for the water is fairly deep immediately offshore and the boulders are large and numerous. The lie appears to extend from a big treetrunk 20 yards below the head of the pool, right down to a toe-toe bush only feet from the rapids at the tail. An odd snag here and there can be annoying, but it is seldom that you will return from the Duchess without a fish or two, and that is the test of any good holding water.

The Silly

The Silly Pool can be fished from either bank, although from the left, to which access is gained through the Hatchery, one is limited to the lower half of the pool only. A high bluff bars the way further upstream.

My own preference is for the right bank, where although casting can be difficult in the extreme because of a high bank topped with lupin, I have had some excellent sport. The head of the pool presents no problems. A pleasant sandy beach gives way to a sandbar which can be followed downstream for about 15 yards by wading, and it is unusual to chalk up a nil return in this area. Again a cast downstream and across—say 30 degrees below the right-angle—seems to sink sufficiently and still manages to avoid a particularly annoying snag which by now must be worth its weight in trout flies. Make your cast directly across river and the odds are 10 to 1 you'll add to the collection.

There is a deep channel close into the bank on the right-hand side and this extends well down the length of the Silly. Look for a large tree stump half way down the pool and high on the stones and have this at your back when you start to cast. Now you can revert to a throw directly across the current without much chance of being snagged. Once you have hooked one in this lower reach of the pool you'll have a particularly torrid fight on your hands as the water is relatively fast and the trout seem to use it to telling effect.

Unless you are confident of your ability to make a steeple cast or a change of direction cast with relative ease, forget about fishing the Silly from the right bank. There is something disheartening about retrieving one's fly from lupin bushes every 20 seconds or so.

The Birches

Both the Upper and Lower Birch pools are fishable from the left-hand bank only. Though I have no doubts whatsoever that the upper holds fish, for the water is fierce from here up to the Silly and the trout will certainly rest before making the ascent, I can't catch a fish in it no matter how I try. Certainly I do not fish it often, but on each occasion that I have worked the Silly Pool from the Hatchery side, I have wandered down to the Upper Birch and given it half an hour. I have the feeling that its depth, especially at the head of the pool, is too great to allow my fly to submerge to the lie of the trout. Four ounces of lead sinker might do the trick, but it is a little too close to the Hatchery and the rangers to give one confidence in illegalities.

The Lower Birch, though not a large body of water, does hold fish and it is not particularly difficult to encourage them to strike. It is a pool which should be fished fairly shallow; that is making the cast at about 45 degrees downstream. The trout are evenly spread throughout the top two thirds of the pool, and if I were to have my choice, I'd enter it about 15 yards down from the head. You won't get a limit out of it, but it is usually good for a fish or two, and the walk through the Hatchery grounds is a bonus of which I never tire.

Cattle Rustlers'

Though not what it was a couple of years ago, when an electric fence upstream caused a massing of fish in the pool, Cattle Rustlers' is still, on its day, productive water to fish. Once again, it is not the ideal pool for the novice, for one must stand with a high bank of stones behind and the ever-encroaching lupins seem determined to snare every wayward cast. Cattle Rustlers' is a pool where one gets value for money. The longer the cast, the more opportunity there is to obtain a strike, for the fairly shallow stony bar down the centre of the pool divides the lie in two. Real shooting-head country this, for if you can hit the far bank with your cast, chances are excellent that the fast-sinking head will provide a strike on that side of the bar. Your prospective return is therefore doubled. Probably the two best lies occur when the angler is standing at the head of the pool and casting 30 degrees downstream. Straight across, and the line is picked up in the swirling current as the river rebounds from the cliff face opposite, and finishes back under one's feet. Make the slightly downstream cast, however, and the line will hesitate for perhaps 30 seconds, allowing the fly to sink and then move beautifully slowly through the width of the pool. Throughout its path, I never fail to have an expectant sensation that any moment there will be that momentary hesitation which signals the unhurried slurp of an unwary trout. It was from this corner that in one of the most remarkable circumstances I have encountered on the river, a trout was successfully hooked and landed.

I mentioned earlier the amusing and frustrating experiences I had weathered at the Red Hut Pool with an American TV film crew. The next pool which caught their eye as being photogenic was Cattle Rustlers' and, as usual, the Star's father-in-law-cum-manager accompanied us. Also, as usual, he had had his customary few vodkas

The feminine angle: Josephine takes an unwary one from Cattle Rustlers' Pool.

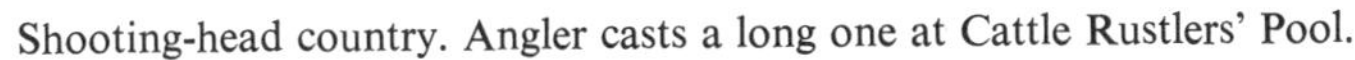

Shooting-head country. Angler casts a long one at Cattle Rustlers' Pool.

for breakfast, or instead of breakfast, I forget which. We handed him a rod, the director moved him off-camera to the head of the pool, and everyone promptly forgot about him as the serious business of the day began. Probably because of the lack of action, father-in-law was brightening his day with a fairly regular nip from his hip flask. The inevitable visit to the undergrowth became necessary and he beached his rod and departed. Now any fisherman worthy of the name would put his line on to his reel at such a time, but father-in-Law, was to say the least, far from being a fisherman. Indeed if A were top mark for angling ability he merited nothing better than Z minus. Comfort stop visited, he returned, had a short one to keep the germs away and picked up his rod. Perhaps the last nip had helped his vocal chords, for there was nothing short of panic in his yell demanding assistance.

His visit had been of sufficient duration for line, leader and fly to be caught up in the swirl. Round and round they had gone, totally bemusing a fish which must have become giddy watching the performance. A split second after he had recorked his flask and was in the process of groping for his rod, she had decided to end the nonsense.

He landed her by a process of constantly reeling and not giving an inch, and spent the remainder of his visit pointing out to me water which, in his estimation, should be full of trout for the taking. For my part I was happy that he had returned when he did, or assuredly I would have been one rod, reel and line the fewer. Further, I should never have believed his story.

Further down the pool is the second lie, which extends from a big stone on the far bank for 30 yards downstream. Here, make the cast straight across the current and during the swing of the fly, hold the rod tip high above your head to keep the belly out of the backing of the shooting-head. In the lower part of Cattle Rustlers', most strikes occur when the fly has moved through almost to the casting side, and the first few pulls of the retrieve often produce a fish. But let me repeat: if you are not a competent caster, this is not the pool for you, and you would do well to save yourself the half-hour walk which is necessary to reach it.

The Stag

There is not a great deal which can be said about the Stag Pool. It is a wide body of water which can be fished from either bank. My preference inclines once again to the right bank, in the main because

Mike Henderson traps one for dinner at Cattle Rustlers'.

of the ease of wading. The left is extremely restricted because of deep water almost to the riverbank. From the right however an angler can move well out into the stream where, typical of so many pools in the Tongariro system, a fairly shallow shingle bar permits fish to be taken from either side. It is possible to wade almost the entire length of the Stag along this bar and enjoy good sport at any section of it. Unlike so many other pools, this one does not appear to contain a couple of favourite lies for resting trout, but is likely to produce a strike anywhere at any time. Fish it deep on the left-hand side as you wade down, and shallower on the right.

A splendid but exhausting day can be had during the spawning season by starting at Red Hut and fishing in succession the Silly, Cattle Rustlers', and the Stag. All, you will have noted, fish better from the right bank, and although the walking is quite extensive, the journey between each pool will enable you to thaw out after an hour or so of extremely cold-water wading.

The Admiral's

Downstream from the Stag the river breaks, with the small tributary clinging to the cliff of the right bank and the main body turning sharp left and cascading rapidly down towards the Admiral's Pool. From the high bank above, it is possible to see fish lying in the quiet pools of the smaller stretch, and if approached with the caution one would normally show on a small stream, they can be encouraged to take. Remember though to keep well back from the water for the first few casts, for often they are lying close in and at the first sight of a two-legged intruder will disappear and cannot again be coaxed to action.

In the river proper the Admiral's is a goodlooking though rather fast pool behind some tall poplar trees. I often try it, but if my success or failure were to be judged by results, I should attain a low marking. An occasional fish, yes, but all too infrequently. Spare a cast or two, however, for the confluence of the two waters downstream a further 50 yards. Try casting into the racing current on your left and wait with bated breath as the fly moves just into the peaceful water of the slow-moving tributary.

I was witness to a strange feat at this spot a year or two ago. Russell Turner, my longtime friend from Napier, was visiting us for a couple of days and, finding the more popular pools a little overcrowded, we had moved upstream. Coming to the glide below the Admiral's I suggested Russell wet a line. He cast into the rapid, let it swing into the more peaceful run and immediately struck a fish. It came out of the water three times in as many seconds, bright red stripe and gill flaps showing. A jack of perhaps 5 lb. Russell fought it hard for about three minutes and then exclaimed "It's gone. I felt it go."

"Bad luck," I said, "it was a good fish too."

Without more ado his rod tip whipped down again and Russell let out a whoop. "No, he's still there," he said, "Darned thing must have been coming straight at me."

The fish exploded from the water and I looked disbelievingly at a silver streak without a touch of red to mar her fresh-run beauty. He had hooked and eventually landed a perfectly formed female of no more than 4 lb only a couple of seconds after losing his jack. He fished the lie for another hour, convinced that there must be fish queued up just waiting for a fly to pass by. If there were others, they had learned their lesson, for not another touch was forthcoming.

The Neverfail

At the top of the Boulevard is a little pool which I like to call the

Neverfail. For many months, though I visited it regularly, it lived up to its name too. To reach it, park your car at the entrance to the Hydro Pool opposite the little Mangamawhitiwhiti outlet and march your way upstream over the boulders for 100 yards or so. There is then a well-trodden path which is easy to follow which terminates in four steps which lead you to the water. Cross the shallow backwater to the stony island slightly downstream of your entrance and start fishing with a very short line where several tiny rivulets join the main stream at the head of the pool. Remain well back from the water about to be fished, for often I have had a fish take with little more than my leader in the water. Proceed once through the pool without getting your feet wet, and on the second time through wade it as deeply as you possibly can.

It is an easy pool to work and is, I think, one of the most consistent producers. Ideally, it is a one-rod pool, for there are only 40 yards of fishable water, but it is a place of great beauty and serenity. Unless everyone who has read this book decides to attack it on the same day, it is unlikely that you will be troubled by others during your couple of quiet hours.

The Hydro

The Boulevard moves purposefully down into the Hydro Pool about half a mile upstream of the river crossing which allows one access to the Major Jones pool. Four years ago the authorities became concerned about the volume of water which was being forced against the left bank and endangering the properties downstream in the event of a major flood. Bulldozers created a diversion to spread the flow down two channels, and almost immediately the Hydro became one of the most consistent producers of fish on the river system. The majority fished it in the obvious way, from the left bank. Others either roll-cast from the right or by use of axe and slasher created sufficient backcasting room just below the entrance of the Mangamawhitiwhiti Stream. Everyone caught fish, and the angler who could cast 80 feet was doubly rewarded.

Gradually, however, a diminishing return became evident with each successive season and this year the pool has been, to say the least, disappointing. I have the feeling that far less water is now proceeding through the new diversion than was the case when it was first completed, although I have no photographic evidence to support this theory.

"All but", or, "Never count your chickens!" This one got away.

Should any of the local residents downstream of the Hydro share my opinion, perhaps they will again make representation to the appropriate authority to counter the flood risk, thus once more establishing the pool as a splendid supplier of trout?

Three years ago I had foisted upon me a cocker spaniel of impeccable pedigree, gentle disposition and a clean bill of health. That she also was completely lacking in canine grey matter and had a most unspaniel-like fear of water, I did not discover until later.

Determined to eradicate this latter trait, having despaired of the former, I drove her to the Hydro, carried her out and gently placed the quivering, whining bundle into the water. There was a flurry of panic before instinct took over and, confidently enough, she made for shore. That, I decided, was enough for one day, and proceeded to get on with the serious business of fishing.

Delight and surprise were equally divided a few minutes later when a bobbing black head appeared at my side, turned, and again headed for the beach. She had, I decided, adopted water as a playground.

Three times she visited in the next half hour and on each occasion, I patted the head as it passed and made appropriate noises of approval.

The fierce whack of a fresh-run fish as it struck banished all further thoughts of moving with confidence into the animal training world, and I concentrated on the battle ahead. A sparkling silver acrobat leapt three feet from the water and, ripping line from the reel, hurtled itself downstream. A female, I decided, 6 lb at least. The reel stopped its scream, suddenly, and my heartbeat slowed. "It's gone," I thought, and started to strip line. Almost in front of me there was an eruption of droplets of water and for a second I could see not only the leader but the fly in her mouth. Unable to pull free on the first made rush she had tried another ploy and had headed back upstream like the White Rabbit of *Alice in Wonderland* fame. Frantically reefing in slack with my left hand, for to attempt to reel in line would have been disastrously slow, I again felt her weight and breathed easier. That last jump had revealed as beautiful a fish as I had hooked in months, and though she would regain her freedom after I had landed her, I wanted the pride of conquest: 7 lb? perhaps even 8? O, she was big, and deep, and fit to be tied.

In one tearing, leaping, impossibly fast run she dragged another 40 yards of line away from me, then sounded and lay collecting her strength. I applied a little more pressure and gained 10 feet of line. Another run, shorter this time, without the same shocking-power. Slowly I gained the supremacy, gaining foot after foot, until, still with a flurry of desperation, she floated on her side, mouth gasping. Yes, I thought, at least 8 lb. Gradually, I eased my way toward the bank, towing my lovely trout on a still firm but short line. She felt the shallower water under her and flapped wildly. I turned to ensure she was still mine, took another step backwards—and fell over my gleefully swimming spaniel. Even as I swore from my sitting position my waders filled with icy water. No good to look to see if the trout were still there. The rod was pointing skywards without the suggestion of a bend, the leader, flyless, mocking me.

I looked around, still sitting. Lisa had just shaken the water from her coat and her tail was a blurred movement of delight. I swear to this day she was grinning.

The Birches swingbridge is more often than not called the Major Jones bridge. If one mentions the former, the reaction is one of surprise that a new one has been established from the Hatchery grounds to the eastern bank of the river, crossing at either the Upper or Lower Birch pools. What the newcomer may not realise, is that the bridge was named after the property of Mr H. N. V. Boulton, whose lovely and extensive gardens are surrounded by the trees.

The Breakfast

A hundred or so yards below the bridge, the Breakfast Pool is easily distinguished. I do not intend to dwell too much upon it, except to say that the head of the pool is often good for a fish or two and that the lower 30 yards will often produce. Fish it, obviously enough, from the left-hand bank and fish it fairly shallow, especially in the bottom half, or rocks and snags will take toll of your fly supply.

CHAPTER 8

FROM MAJOR JONES TO THE BRIDGE

MAJOR JONES: the name is synonymous with the greatness of the Tongariro River. Probably, if it were not so over-populated at the height of the season it would be everyone's favourite, and despite the number of rods it is still the first choice of many overseas and local anglers. It has so many attributes to make it a fisherman's dream come true. It has depth. It is, by far, the longest pool of the river. Despite flood and drought it remains virtually changeless. Yielding fish to the skilled, it will still be kind to the inexperienced or inexpert. It is an easy pool to wade.

The far or left-hand bank is a kaleidoscope of colour provided by native and exotic trees and shrubs.

Major Jones is, simply, a great pool and I do not use the adjective lightly. Admiral Hickling expressed his preference for the upper reach of the Major and I think that up until four or five years ago, this opinion was well founded. Nowadays I am convinced that the area from the first big rock on the far bank down to the water-level pole is the hottest spot on the river. A good caster using for preference a shooting head, can count himself unfortunate indeed if he fishes these 30 yards unprofitably. By casting straight across the current to the western bank, immediately sinking the fly by mending an additional 5 or 10 yards of line, the path of the lure is slow and deep. Chances are that as the fly straightens up directly below the fisherman or on the first couple of pulls of the retrieve, the action will begin—and what action there can be when a big run of fish is holding in the pool! My own record was established in this same position in June 1971. Eight successive casts for 8 successive strikes. My diary, ecstatic in its description of a superlative morning's fishing, tells me I landed 5 of those 8 and had landed and released 12 by 10 am. That, in anyone's language, in anyone's country, just has to be magnificent fishing.

There is no special secret to catching fish in the Major. Enter the pool opposite the concrete culvert, fish it deep and work your way

"Father, Mother and the Niece who came to dinner". Three splendid Tongariro rainbows.

through it thoroughly. Useless to suggest that you approach it as I like to fish any pool; that is, wading shallow the first time through and deep on the next, for the four or five fellows in front or behind will have plunged in to the plimsoll line of their waders as soon as they arrived. Just how many fish, notably shallow-lying browns, are driven into heavy water by the first mad rush of early morning anglers, we shall never know. From experience on other pools, which can be worked at leisure without competition, scores of readily available trout must escape to relative safety. Probably the first man through doesn't realise it, but he is, in fact, practising conservation. So maybe it's all for the common good.

Advice and help are often volunteered from an unusual source. Those fortunates who dwell on the western bank of the pool regularly wander down "to see how the fishing is" and generally greet a new arrival with "They took a lot of fish this morning," or, if it happens to be morning, "You should have been here last evening. So-and-so got his limit in two hours."

It is possible that you might have only a couple of rods for competition at 6 o'clock in the morning, but these days it is surprising if fewer than six or eight anglers are not jockeying for position at any given time of the day. Of a consequence I do not fish the Major as much as I should like, for I have no great love of crowds when on the river. A good companion, an occasional strike to keep the adrenalin coursing and as much possible distance separating us from the rest of humanity is my idea of bliss.

Perhaps it is because of the crowding that many of us have detected a selfishness among some of the regulars who fish the Major Jones. There is a code of etiquette on most rivers which the greater majority observe. The incoming fisherman enters the pool at its head, or at least upstream of any other rod already in the pool.

He makes only a few casts and proceeds a couple of paces downstream. A few more casts and so on.

If each rod in the pool complies with the pattern, there is harmony, but let just one individual check the remainder, and friction is inevitable. I guided a client a year or more ago who gave a local and wellknown water hog a lesson he might well have taken to heart. We had fished both Red Hut and the Island pools in the morning, and though he had taken fish in both, he was limited to only two days of fishing on his tour of New Zealand and was anxious to see as much water as his time would allow. I suggested that if there were not too many in the Major that he might do well to try it. He agreed and off we went. There were only two fellows working as we arrived, and I led my man out to the head of the pool. He made a few casts and, as an observer of the niceties, moved down a couple of paces. Within a quarter of an hour he was nearly rubbing shoulders with his downstream neighbour, who showed no sign of moving.

My client gave me an enquiring look, I indicated that he should move even closer, and we both waited for the ignorant one to get the message. He stayed put.

There is one way of approaching types like this which does not lead to open warfare, and I questioned him.

"Are you moving down, sir, or would you like us to move around and below you?"

"I'm moving," he said, and changed his position all of six inches. "But I was here first and I'm not going to rush."

I kept my temper in check, shrugged my shoulders at my client, and waited for the inevitable. I should mention here that my client was an Australian of enormous proportions and an admittedly uncertain disposition. He was getting slightly red of countenance. I rejoined

Englishman Tavish Thomson-Moore poses with justifiable pride beside the Major Jones Pool.

One of the world's great trout pools. Anglers working their way through Major Jones.

him, mouthing—I hoped—sweet and soothing reasonableness, but he was not to be placated.

"Rude bastard, isn't he?" he said, just sufficiently quietly to be heard half a mile downstream. "Well, he'd better get moving or I'm going to know the reason why!" He started casting furiously.

The slowcoach was not to be intimidated. At a guess, I'd say he moved about 4 inches every 10 minutes.

"I've met these blokes before on previous visits," said my client in his gentle roar. "I'll show you how we move them."

Before I could dissuade him from whatever drastic action he had eventually decided to take, he proceeded to cast with a very flat, very low, very fast action. That shooting-head with its no. 4 hook was passing only inches above the head of the fellow downstream and he took hasty evasive measures. Looking up warily from his crouched position he asked in a tone best described as truculent, "Just what the hell my man are you doing?"

"I'm trying to make a sportsman out of you," he was told. "I'm trying to teach you the etiquette of the river. I'm trying to get you to move down and let someone else have a crack at the pool. And I'll tell you something else, mate, I'm going to do it too. If that little exhibition of fancy casting doesn't impress you into getting your posterior into gear, I've got another couple of tricks up my sleeve. Firstly, I make sure on my very next cast that I hook your waders with the biggest fly in the box. That'll get them leaking nicely. And if that fails to work the oracle, I use the last method. I push you in and hold you under until there are no more bubbles coming to the surface."

Throughout this outrageous outburst I was wishing I could find a hole, jump in and pull it in after me. I had, over the years, heard a few exchanges on the river, but nothing to match this. Neither, obviously, had the poor recipient of this torrent of threats. He hastily reeled in his line, moved quickly toward the bank and disappeared from view. He reappeared a few moments later, however, to shout, "Hope you never catch a fish, you —. And I hope you fall in." He received one of his wishes too. We didn't take a fish out of the Major throughout that afternoon.

All this unpleasantness could have been avoided if the etiquette of the river had been maintained and recognised. Strangely, there are only three pools on the river which seem to attract the water hog. Cattle Rustlers' was a shocking example when the electric barrier was functioning upstream and the pool was full of fish plucking up courage to move through it. The angling gannets occupied the best lies from dawn till dark and no amount of persuasion or impassioned blasphemy could move them. Red Hut has its share on occasion, usually when they are fishing the lie halfway down the pool. Here they come to almost a complete stop and take an hour or more to move the next 10 or 15 yards.

My good friend and possibly the most popular regular visitor to our area, Fred Goddard of Seattle, spends one month of every year fishing the Tongariro and his great love is the Major Jones Pool. Fred is undeniably an expert angler but perhaps even more importantly, he is one of nature's gentlemen. Because of his skill he takes more than his share of fish, but he is always willing to help a new chum with advice and he observes the manners of the river to the letter. Coupled with his natural charm, his popularity is well deserved. He and I were fishing in friendly rivalry one morning in June 1972. Ahead of us were two men who, despite our entry to the pool at 6 o'clock on a frosty morning, had preceded us. Fred moved in opposite the culvert and I waited for 10 minutes before following him down. By 7 o'clock we were marking time halfway down the pool while the two early arrivals, spaced 20 yards apart, seemed to have come to a dead stop. It took us until 11.30 am to work our way down to the large stone lie at the bottom, by which time neither of us was in a particularly good humour. We had said nothing, despite an overpowering urge to remonstrate.

"Perhaps they're only here for the day, and want to take a few fish back," suggested Fred in his kindly way.

"Let's hope so," I replied. "Anyway, we'll get down earlier tomorrow morning just in case."

Two hours before dawn, we appeared the following morning. Frost crackled underfoot as we marched urgently from the footbridge to the pool. Pitch black. Fingers numb already. Probing torches revealed no other form, nor had there been a car in the park where we had left Fred's hired Vauxhall.

"We're first here, all right," I said. "Let's have a cup of coffee to warm us up before we start."

We had taken only a sip when the murmur of the river which was the only sound around us was broken.

"Got one!" said a voice, a voice we knew only too well.

Again we fumed and fretted our snailpaced way through the pool.

Above left: Beauty with two beauties from the Major Jones.
Above Right: The author with a fine 8-pounder taken from Major Jones.

At 10 o'clock and only halfway down, I'd had enough. I reeled in, moved down the bank and approached the leading tortoise.

"Good morning," I greeted him. "My friend and I are pleased to see you having some luck in the lie, but do you think you could move through a little faster so that we may all have a crack at it?" By now there were seven rods in the Major and five of them were far from happy.

"There's plenty of other water in the Tongariro if you don't like the pace," I was told, and he proceeded to cast again, without budging an inch.

It is rare to encounter this sort of rebuff among the gentlemen and gentlewomen of the river, and for once in my life I was left speechless. I certainly did not want to enter into a slanging match as my Australian client had done, and I was also aware that the slowcoach was my height and about three stone heavier. I muttered something about spoiling the day for others and, being ignored, returned up river and took my place.

For a solid week those two monopolised the Major Jones pool. They were nicknamed Lightning and Rigor Mortis by all and sundry, and despite constant loud references to their new names, made no effort to mend their ways. It was a shock to learn a day or so before their departure that they were members of that august body which supposedly has the best interests of Taupo fishing at heart—Taltac (Tongariro and Lake Taupo Anglers' Club).

No wonder they required no car. The club rooms and lodge where they were staying are only a stone's throw from the river crossing. It would be too much to hope that both these fellows should read this chapter, but in the unlikely event that they do, let us hope thay recognise themselves and feel a pang of conscience. When all is said and done, fishing for trout is a sport and recreation, not a business of killing fish greedily and in an unsportsmanlike manner.

The Island

Below Major Jones the river divides at the Island Pool, with the main body of water favouring the right bank. Quite a volume, however, flows down a narrow entrance on the left side. From this small pool, I have limited success in normal conditions, but following a rise in the river, it is full of fish.

Short casting only is necessary, dropping the fly within inches of the far bank and letting it swing naturally until it is immediately below the rod tip. During flood or fresh, trout naturally seek a fairly protected spot to rest away from the hard battle of the main current, and this little glide seems to fulfil that requirement.

The Island Pool proper used to be a wonderful producer for me until three years ago, but of late I count myself lucky to land a couple of trout in a morning's fishing. I have the impression that it has become more shallow and consequently less attractive to the large numbers of fish which used to rest there. It is a pool where deep wading is advantageous, for the lie, though fairly evenly dispersed throughout the length of the pool, seems to extend from right against the eastern or right bank only out from it for 10 or 15 feet. There is a large blackberry bush on the eastern bank which overhangs into the water, and this lie seems to hold more trout than anywhere in the pool. A cast of about 60 feet is required at this point, so it is not difficult for even a moderate caster to land his fly just upstream of the bush.

The riverbed changes to some extent after a really big flood, and I hope sincerely that the Island will reestablish itself as one of the great pools of the river in the not-too-far-distant future. Not, mark you, that we want a repeat of that terrifying 1958 flood which altered so many of the pools as to make them unrecognisable. Besides which, Jo and I live so close to the river that a repetition of that one would no doubt fill our bedroom with water. Ever tried catching trout in your own hallway?

The Lonely

The current downstream of the island is particularly strong and does not yield spectacularly until it reaches the Lonely Pool. A long pool, clearly visible upstream from the No. 1 Highway bridge, it fishes extremely well in its headwaters and will, in fact, provide good angling almost throughout its length. Access to the Lonely is a little difficult for older anglers or the infirm, for it requires quite a scramble first up and then down the cliff face on the northern side of the bridge. Once this is achieved, good fishing is pretty well assured if there has been a run in the river. At the head cast quite short—say 20 feet only—while standing back from the water, and gradually increase the length with each individual throw. Try casting slightly upstream and across so that the fly and leader at least land in the white water above the slack. In doing this, it is amazing how often the first cast of the day will give you a strike and boost your confidence for the remaining hours. Twenty-two yards below the head of the pool there is a deep hole, only about 10 feet in diameter and 20 feet long which, on occasion, must hold literally hundreds of fish. It is a fairly easy pool to wade until one approaches the tail, where the water gathers speed and balance becomes rather precarious.

I use the shallow side of the Groin Pool above the Bridge as my barometer for the river. If, while standing on the bridge you can see a dozen or more fish lying in the shallows, you may assure yourself that there is a good run of trout throughout the river. I'm satisfied that having been seen so often leaning over the parapet, people must decide that I am considering self-destruction without ever quite being able to pluck up the courage.

CHAPTER 9

THE LOWER REACHES

IT IS NOT MY INTENTION, you will no doubt be delighted to know, to enter into a yard-by-yard description of the Tongariro below the No. 1 Highway bridge. There are, when all said and done, over 5 miles of winding river from the Bridge to the Delta and though I have fished it all and still retain a couple of favourite spots which I work regularly, there is much flat, undefined water upon which the reader may care to experiment on his own.

Many of the easily recognisable pools of past years appear to have become silted to a relatively even depth and in my experience, possibly because of the moving bottom, the trout do not lie in them any longer than is necessary. Even such a short distance downstream as Down's Pool, once so popular and a splendid producer, the sand and pumice have covered much of the pebbly bottom. Whether the removal of so much stone for crushing released the sediment, I am not prepared to hazard a guess, but certainly the downstream fishing has deteriorated from the Reed Pool down, and even the Reed is but a shadow of its former self.

Let's have a look however, in pencil-sketch form at the odd stretches which will yield for you, some of them surprisingly well if you know where the lies are.

The Bridge Lodge

Bridge Pool, or Bridge Lodge Pool as it is more often termed these days, did not fish nearly as well during the 1972 season as it has done in the past. I quite simply do not know the answer either, because it changed practically not at all in feature. It has always been the very devil of a pool to wade, with round, exceedingly slippery stones packed close together defying the angler to obtain a thoroughly balanced foothold. I have not fallen over often in the Tongariro, but I did succeed twice in three days in Bridge Lodge pool. It was in July, too, when the water was snow-fed. I still shiver at the memory.

Hopefuls fishing the rip above the Birches swingbridge.

There used to be a thoroughly splendid lie just below the bridge itself. The object was to wade across two deep guts of fairly slack water and position yourself as close to the middle pylon as possible. It wasn't even necessary to cast if you were far from expert; just feed out 30 or 40 feet of line, let it sink, and retrieve. I've tried it twenty or more times over the past seasons for limited success, and yet it looks just the same as it did in 1971, when it never failed to give excitement.

The trout are the only ones who know the reason, and they're not about to publicise it.

Twenty yards below the bridge there is an outcrop of exposed rocks forming a tiny island and most anglers begin casting from here, methodically working their way down the length of the pool. Fish are fairly evenly scattered throughout.

The opposite or northern bank is fished quite extensively too, and offers good fishing following a rise in the river. A change of direction cast or a roll cast is necessary while the fisherman is under the 10-foot bank, but further down wading is not too difficult and it is possible to move out sufficiently far to cast normally.

As the current leaves Bridge Lodge it angles left through a series of tiny wadeable rapids and follows the left bank closely for 100 yards or so before colliding with the clay bank and turning right to form Swirl Pool.

The Swirl

Again, following a noticeable fresh in the Tongariro, the small body of water adjacent to the bank and fed by the small rapids will provide good sport, although once hooked every fish seems to have one thought in mind: he turns immediately, heading downstream and uses the fast flowing current to full effect, tearing line from the reel at an alarming rate. Seldom do they turn easily and, knowing the pitfalls, I now use 2 or 3 lb breaking strain more on my leader than in most other pools on the river. It's fun, but I'll make a small wager that you'll land only one in three unless you're using monofilament which is built for an anchor warp.

The Swirl looks as if it would hold a great number of fish in its headwaters. Perhaps it does, but the pool is aptly named and I doubt, with the circular water movement, whether one's fly ever looks realistic to a fish lying deep. It is no criterion, but I can't pull one out of that disturbed water. Further down the pleasant, sandy beach however it is a different story and, though you will not take a limit from the lower reaches they will usually provide a fish or two. I use it quite regularly for a guest's breakfast fish, as it is only a couple of hundred yards from my house and seems to fish better in the early morning than at any other time of the day.

The Stones

Down river of the Swirl are 200 yards or more where the river widens considerably. Running parallel with Herekiekie Street, it is approached through a right-of-way two thirds of the way down that road. Often called the Stones, it is aptly named, for wading, except in the headwaters, is both unwise and fruitless. Unwise, because of the strength of the current and fruitless because a high stony bank at one's back is invited to barb a hook the further out one moves. Personally, I know of a hundred other spots I should much prefer to fish, but I do not deny that it yields some fantastic catches at times.

You will need to keep your right arm quite vertical through your backcast, for besides the stone bank the ever-encroaching lupins add an additional 4 feet to the height your fly must surmount. Take care too, where you place your feet on the slope of the bank. Many of the

"And what do you think of that?" Dr Ron Kennedy looks delighted with his rainbow.

stones are not firmly embedded and a rolling one will throw you, often painfully. Both sides of the river will deliver fish, but the eastern bank is my preference, and by the number of anglers at regular intervals along its shore during the season, I am not alone in my assessment.

As mentioned earlier, the tremendous and frightening flood of 1958 altered practically every feature of the Tongariro. No arca suffered more than that section which incorporated the Hut, Log, Stump, Boat, The Crossing and Nursery pools. The river here was devastated and became unrecognisable. To the hardy and perennial fisherman, the loss of the Hut, in particular, was a tragedy. A mighty pool, generous in its bounty, had gone for ever. There were those who fished no other waters of the river, who knew every stone, who could recount tales of the past 40 years and for whom the desecration of the Hut was a major disaster. And so it was. What remained was a wide, uninteresting flow of steadily moving water, difficult to fish and, partly for that same reason, giving up only an occasional trout.

Enter the pundits and the introduction of the electric power scheme. Rock for crushing was necessary and despite cries of protest from every angler worth his salt, it was finally determined to dredge this same water for the purpose.

Firstly the Tongariro had to be diverted, and to this end a 40-yard-wide channel was constructed of perhaps three quarters of a mile in length. It was, to say the least, unimaginative, for it was built as straight as an arrow throughout its length and, until two or three floods had obliged by forming a remote resemblance to pools, was of quite uniform depth. Enormous and greedy snags plucked away flies from leaders or leaders from lines with regular monotony and the mutterings and mumblings could be heard throughout its length. Perhaps because of the many resting places behind the snags, however, the channel did fish remarkably well, and though one would return with a pathetically reduced number of favourite fly patterns, it was seldom that one came away emptyhanded.

Meantime, the heavy machinery did its work in the dry riverbed, until, in April of last year, the Tongariro was again diverted to its original banks. Our interested gaze revealed a wide expanse of slow-moving water, more extensive indeed than any section of the Tongariro from its source to its mouth.

I remember sighing aloud and saying to Trevor Thompson, who had joined me, "It'll take about a dozen good floods through this before we can find the lies."

His reply was typical: "They've got to move through it to get further upstream, so you'll just have to search until you find the lies."

It was to be a formidable task, for the river here was, in parts, 80 yards across, unbroken by white water and pitted with holes left by the excavations. Much of it near the western bank was nothing but soft, clinging mud upon which no self-respecting fish would lie.

It took me every spare moment over a couple of months to gain some knowledge of the movement of the trout as they forged their way upstream. Finally a pattern began to emerge. Having moved through the Reed Pool downstream, the fish remained close to the left bank until they had travelled a couple of hundred yards upstream. They then angled their way over to the right and proceeded toward the Stones Pool along that side. Let's start from the western or left bank first.

Unless you are familiar with the area, you'll need some directions to take you there. Tautahanga Road virtually encircles the business area and some residential property of Turangi. Driving off Highway 1 turn right having passed the hotel (or having finally left it) and proceed until you see an outdated AA sign directing you to the now defunct pools mentioned earlier. Continue down a dirt road, currently a labyrinth of potholes, bearing left all the way, until you meet another rough road. Turn sharp right and continue eastward until you are nearly in the river. Another left turn here and follow the Tongariro. Four hundred yards will lead you to a position from where you can see a small stone and sand island almost exactly in the middle of the stream. Make your muddy crossing from immediately opposite this small outcrop and begin fishing the obviously deep channel from 10 yards above the island to a point 25 yards below it. Go further and your only reward will be wet waders, for it drops away quite suddenly.

A word of warning here to the unwary if I may: don't fish this lie if the river is cloudy and the bottom invisible. There are too many holes for comfort and some of them are deceptively deep. To the best of my knowledge, no one has as yet suggested a name for this body of water and mentally I think of it as the Lower Island Pool. That's fine—until the next flood either removes the island permanently or changes the lie.

Further down and opposite three large exposed rocks two thirds of the way to the far shore, there is shallow water which can be crossed by moving at a 45-degree angle downstream. Following it, only when the water is clear, is easy. There is deep water on both sides of this 6-foot-wide, knee-high path which allows you access to 60 yards of fishable river. The right bank is the more productive. One recommendation here: I rarely carry a net with me on the Tongariro, but towing a fish perhaps 50 yards to the shore is both a waste of time and allows the fish much more opportunity to free itself. Having netted it, you may string it from your belt if you decide to keep it.

The Log

Another hundred yards down the road will bring you to a stump on the water's edge. Deep water is evident immediately off-shore and if you like to catch fish without the aid of waders, this is the place to satisfy your whim. Some of the locals have named it the Log Pool, after the two large trunks cast high on the bank, but to me it will always be Marie's Pool. I introduced Marie Gilkison to this lie a

Success, followed by smug satisfaction. An angler lands and proudly demonstrates a fresh-run rainbow.

few days after I had discovered it for myself, and her baptism was quite remarkable. She has fished the Taupo area for many years, and though quite tiny and slight of stature she casts an exceptional line for her size, succeeding through quite perfect timing. Having shown her the position where she should stand, I turned to the car which was parked only 10 feet away and commenced to remove my rod from the roof rack.

"I have one," she cried, and almost unbelieving I looked over my shoulder. With her very first cast she had hooked a fresh-run female which, at that moment, was spending more time out of the water than it was in it. Five minutes later I removed the hook for her, admired the fish and returned to the car. I didn't even get that far next time.

"This is too easy," she laughed, and surely enough, her rod was bent almost double as she fought another which had taken her next presentation.

"Give me time at least to get fishing," I implored her, although delighted that she was enjoying the sport. She is quite capable of extracting her own hooks, having had as much practice as half a dozen men combined, but I played the gentleman and performed the task. Another lovely hen fish of more than 5 lb. The next time she did allow me to extract my rod, examine the fly and take two steps upstream before she again called out. For the third time her reel was screaming with the sound that makes an angler's heart skip a beat, and again she landed her fish, a replica of the other two, deep, silver, beautiful.

"I'm getting exhausted," she said, "where's that coffee you brought in the thermos?"

"It's in the car," I told her, "but you can help yourself, I'm going fishing."

I too landed three that afternoon, but they were at least spaced over a couple of hours, while Marie, fishing leisurely, took another couple. She hasn't yet let me forget the day that she had three on the bank before I had completed my preparations. So, Log Pool, or whatever else it is ever called, it will always be to me, Marie's Pool, for shortly after lunch on even a barely fishable day, there you will find her, and rarely will she be without evidence of success. I often fish with her when I have some time to myself, but if I do I know I can expect some stiff competition.

From this stump on the river's edge, it is possible to fish the long glide for as far as one can go downstream, perhaps another 150 yards.

I shall be extremely interested to see the results of a really angry flood on this vast area of water, for since April 1971 we have had nothing of note. Perhaps the island will no longer be evident, and probably the stump will find its way out to the delta. If and when that occurs, it will probably be necessary to re-explore the river at this point and once again find the new lies. But that's fun in itself, and

Gymnastics extraordinary. Marie Gilkison lands a dandy from her favourite Log Pool.

there's a great feeling of satisfaction when you pull a few good ones out of a newly-formed hole.

The opposite bank fishes pretty well too, although the hot spot extends for only about 50 yards. Drive down Grace Road and take the left-hand turn opposite the now-defunct Fletcher's Mill.

The road runs right to the river and a convenient siding leaves room to park the car. Wade across a narrow gut of water until once again you find a shallow path of rocks with deep water evident beyond. It is possible to follow this track downstream at little more than knee depth. It is quite probable that there are other lies which, as yet, I have not discovered, so, with respect for the deep holes left by excavations, have a ferret around this section of river on your own some time. But if you do find an outstanding lie, don't forget to keep me informed, will you?

The Reed

The Reed Pool just ain't wot it used to be, and is restricted to two regularly consistent lies. Fishing from the left bank, the tail of the pool is surprisingly deep as the current channels in against a grassy bank. If you are fortunate enough to have first use of it, you will, in all probability, pick up a fish or two, and on one memorable occasion in April of this year, a client of mine snagged no fewer than seven fresh-run rainbows in not much more than an hour. That's fishing with a capital F.

Thirty yards below this lie the river gathers itself and hurtles against a bank overgrown with large willows. It wasn't until I saw a young lad pull three fish out of this unlikely-looking run that I realised its potential. He didn't cast particularly well, which was not surprising, as he was using a baitcasting rod with an enormous 5-inch trolling reel attached. A cotton line, similar to that used by children when rock fishing was wound on to the reel, in defiance of all the accepted principles of high density equipment, and his leader could have been used as a substitute for no. 8 fencing wire.

"Do you fish here much?" I asked him.

"Every day of the holidays so far," he replied. The May school vacation had begun ten days previously.

"And how many have you caught in that time?"

"These three make the total forty-one," I was told. Forty-one! That was better than the experts were doing in Major Jones.

"I can't fish the other pools," the boy lamented, "I haven't any waders and the water's too cold to stay in long."

I left him then, and though I let him have undisputed occupancy of the pool, which will take only one rod, for the duration of his holidays, I couldn't wait to investigate it during the following week. Perhaps he was a better fisherman or, because of his limited equipment he was obliged to be more patient, I don't know, but my best return out of the hole has been two fish on a visit. Perhaps he's found a secret with a salt water line . . .?

The fish, incidentally, lie in quite close to the left-hand bank in some placid water which barely seems to move.

From here on down, the Tongariro seems to have developed into a hit-or-miss pattern with long-established pools often refusing to yield, and the features of the same pools gradually changing for the worse.

Jones Pool, into which the Reed flows was ruined in a matter of a week by the excavators, who, having wreaked their devastation, moved on. DeLatour's pool, once a prolific producer of trout, is now virtually unfishable from the right bank. A flood three years ago created a flow which carries one's fly in under the overhanging willows and amongst the innumerable snags which became embedded on the soft bottom.

DeLatour's

I reflect on DeLatour's pool with some nostalgia, for it was here that my wife Jo landed her first, and biggest, Tongariro rainbow. She had decided, quite sensibly, upon arrival in Turangi, to adopt the policy of "when in Rome . . ." and following some casting practice on the lawn, professed herself ready, willing and nearly able to attack the denizens of the deep.

Dressed in a pair of my size 9 waders (for I was not about to purchase a pair for her until I was certain she would persevere) she was, to put it kindly, well protected. The plimsoll line was only just beneath her eyes, and unless she moved with a coolie-like shuffle, she was inclined to lift her feet out of the boots. We parked the car opposite the entrance to Fearon Grace's property and I helped her to ford the river to a small sandbar at the head of the pool.

"Cast there, let it swing, wait thirty seconds and then retrieve as you've been shown," I told her. "But keep your rod tip well out in the current or you'll become snagged on a stump ten yards below."

She had been a good pupil on the lawn and she now demonstrated an aptitude which was quite exceptional when faced with the real thing. Twenty casts later, during which time she had done nothing drastically wrong, and during which period she hadn't had the semblance of a touch, I felt that I had done my duty.

"I'm going to wander upstream, dear, and try the water above," I said. "Just carry on the way you're doing and something could well come along." Such was her concentration, I doubted whether she heard me.

A quarter of an hour later I was working Smallman's Reach when a casual glance in Jo's direction revealed, in the rays of the setting sun, a rod which was noticeably bent. "She's on that snag," I thought. "O well, it'll give her practice in tying on a fly and leader."

Merrily I cast away with singular lack of success, until ten minutes later I again checked on my wife. The rod was still bent, and from Jo's antics there could be only one conclusion. Wading furiously I made the bank and, running as best I could in chest waders through a path impeded with fallen boughs and blackberry, I eventually appeared opposite her.

She was sitting on the sandbar, rod still alarmingly bent, an expression of complete incredulity on her face, and, flapping vigorously between her outstretched legs was a trout. What was more, even from twenty yards away, it was a big one.

I waded across to her.

"Where *were* you?" she wailed. "I yelled. I tried to beckon you. I did everything to attract your attention, but you wouldn't come!"

"Why the panic?" I asked. "You've just succeeded in landing one of the best fish I've seen in months."

She was not to be placated. "You taught me to cast, you taught me how to tie on flies and leaders, you taught me how to play a fish, but not one word did you say about how to land one. I've had this one up to the bank about twenty times, but the rod is so long I couldn't bend in these damned waders far enough to catch hold of it."

"What did you do eventually?"

"I finished up by walking backwards and towing it up on the sand," she said.

"And that's the answer to all your problems," I replied. "And don't you think it's time you removed that Mrs Simpson from this magnificent specimen?"

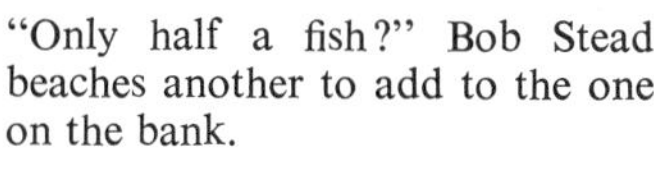

"Only half a fish?" Bob Stead beaches another to add to the one on the bank.

"You do it," she said.

I refused. "If you're going to fish, you won't always have someone around to do your dirty work, so please extract that hook."

She did the job without fuss and then a huge smile broke out. "Not bad for my first effort, is it?"

I gave her a squeeze and agreed wholeheartedly. "Welcome to the ranks of the slightly insane," I said. "From now on you're committed."

The fish weighed $7\frac{3}{4}$ lb, and despite the fact that she has caught hundreds of fish since, it still remains her personal record. Her very first. It shouldn't be allowed. . . .

The Downs and Others

Apart from the likelihood of picking up an enormous brown of a summer evening, providing the mosquitoes have not attacked *en masse*, I find the Downs Pool disappointing in its return these days. On occasion, when there is a big run of trout moving up river, it is possible to collect a couple, but I am certain that it is not being used as a resting pool as once it was. It's a pity, for there is much fishable water here, but whereas you were lucky to have first use of the pool in bygone days, it is rarely now that you will encounter another rod.

Such is the sad story from Downs all the way to the delta. Grace's, The Bend, Poplar, Cherry, all famous in years gone by, are seldom fished, in part because of the difficulties encountered with overhanging willows but, I fear, more especially because so many tiring journeys have been fruitless.

There is no restriction on fishing from an anchored boat up as far as the Downs, and it surprises me that more anglers don't take advantage of the opportunity. A quick run as far as, say, Poplar Pool and all these pools could be worked thoroughly by retrieving the anchor, drifting toward a likely-looking spot and again lowering the anchor. The odds are good that you'd have three miles of water to yourself and give some relief to the overpopulated pools upstream. But don't be tempted to troll your way up, will you? Productive it would be, I have no doubt, but expensive it could be too!

A few fishermen I know still fish the lower reaches of the Tongariro, not because they expect to land as many fish as their counterparts in the better established pools upstream, but to escape the crowded atmosphere which prevails there. I can well understand their attitude too, for there is a serenity about the lower river which is not found elsewhere. Rapids and white water have given way to long, silent glides overhung with basket willow, bare of leaf but golden in the autumn sunshine, deep-green and cool in spring and summer. Brown and rainbow laze contentedly near the banks, seemingly aware of the security offered by the countless snags protecting them, and the tranquillity is disturbed only by the crying of gulls or the hasty departure of wild duck.

The lower Tongariro appealed to Bayard Fox, a fanatical angler from Philadelphia, for two reasons. Although an excellent caster who would take his share of fish from any water, he disliked crowds and, more importantly, he had broken his hip some months before and was compelled to use crutches. I had, naturally enough, prepared the boat and had decided that we should anchor at the Delta where he could sit and cast in relative comfort.

After half an hour he had had enough. "Is there any chance of picking up a fish in the river?" he asked me, looking upstream. "I really don't enjoy fishing from a boat very much."

I looked at his crutches, remembered the overgrown track which he would have to negotiate, took into account that he would have to wade in order to cast, and decided on an evasion of fact. "The odds are against it," I said. "There'll be a few lying around, but they'll be tough to move in the middle of the day."

"I'd sooner take one in the river than ten here," he said. "Let's go and try them anyway."

Resigned to carrying 6 feet 5 inches of brawny client over my shoulder, I beached the boat and prepared for the worst. Little did I know about the sheer guts of the man. Crutches sinking into the mud which turns the trail into a gluey morass, he followed doggedly. Twice he fell, and apart from a muttered curse, not once did he complain. For half a mile he swung himself over fallen logs, negotiated swampy quagmires and half crawled under overhanging branches. Finally, I indicated the junction of the main mouth with the river proper.

"That's your best bet for a fish," I told him, "but you'll have to wade well out to cover the lie."

Guts, did I say? The man was incredible. He plunged into that water, crutches propelled against the current and within minutes he was in position.

"Now," I thought, "let's see you cast!"

He made it look easy. With both crutches under his left arm and firmly embedded in the sand, his right arm was free to manipulate the rod with unimpaired skill, and in a few moments it was possible to forget that he was in any way hampered.

There are tales which deserve a happy ending. Someone Up There admired Bayard's determination and courage and decided they were deserving. Half an hour after he had installed himself, he let out a bellow which could have been heard at the northern end of the lake. "Got one," he yelled, "and I think it's a beauty." By the way his rod was bucking and by the commotion on the water 30 yards downstream, I guessed it was too. The fish came at him fast, and rather than try to pick up line on the reel, he reefed in quickly by hand. The rod was still bent like a green stick. Bayard was busy trying to keep the trout from heaving under the bank and into the snags when he let out another exclamation. "It's gone," he cried.

A glance assured me that the fish was still attached.

"Not the fish," he said "my bloody crutch."

Surely enough, quietly floating away on the gentle current, was his sole means of forward momentum.

"You worry about the fish," I said "I'll worry about the crutch."

Waders are fine for their purpose, but were never designed for creating new records for the 800 metres.

Hurdling, too, I found, was difficult in the extreme as my foot caught on a fallen branch and I measured my length in glutinous mud.

Panting hard, I stopped at a spot which I estimated to be downstream of the escapee. The river here is wide, perhaps 60 yards across, and right in the middle, 100 feet up-river, floated the crutch.

A frantic rush through the shallows, and I was still in time to make the capture, but now the water was within a couple of inches of my wader top, and I was still 5 feet from the path of interception. A moment of hesitation, the dreadful thought of struggling back with Bayard over my shoulder, and I took the last, waterlogged two steps. Mission accomplished, but at what price? Leaden-footed, saturated, the cold already chilling my bones, I stumbled back to shore. There is something belittling about struggling from well-filled waders, examining saturated trousers and socks, stripping down and wringing out and then replacing the cold clammy garments once again. The breeze has an edge to it, previously unnoticed, and you become increasingly aware that the day is only half over and you are far, far from home.

Miserably, slowly, resignedly, I toiled back upstream.

Somehow Bayard had moved back to the little island which guards the pool. In triumph he was holding aloft a female brown trout of perfect proportion which proved to be of 9lb. In the middle of the day! Impossible!

"Did you foul-hook it?" I asked.

He looked hurt. "If I did," he scoffed, "it was caught from behind in the lower jaw."

I had to grin, despite my misery. "Wonderful," I said. "Congratulations. You deserve it."

It was only then that he took in my appearance. "You're all wet," he said, providing the understatement of the year. "Did you do that retrieving my crutch?"

I indicated that his conjecture was indeed correct.

"Gee," he said, "that's rotten luck. I reckoned on staying until after dark too. If I can get a baby like this in the bright sunshine, imagine what we can do once the sun goes down."

Crestfallen, pleadingly, I gazed back at him, teeth already chattering at the thought of the hours to come. I could feel the outcome. The sun disappearing behind the western hills, the first biting breeze of evening, the slipping, sliding progress through the inky blackness to the boat, the numbed hands fumbling at the controls, the icy ride

"How many casts have I made? Two, of course!"

back to the jetty, the onrushing cold, pneumonia, my wife's sobbing acceptance of the inevitable. It was too much.

"Will you promise not to move from where I put you for an hour?" I asked him. "And will you also swear that you'll keep those damned crutches under control?"

He assured me on both points.

"Then I'm going home to change," I said, "and when I get back I shan't mind if you fish until 11 pm."

Do you know what time we made that dark, slipping, sliding return to the boat that night? That's right—11 pm!

I mentioned that the man was a fanatic, but it wasn't until we'd been fishing for three consecutive days from 5 am until 11 pm that I realised just how fanatical he was. On crutches! Four more brownies and one rainbow were landed that first night at an average of just over 7 lb. Believe me, nobody ever deserved them more.

Generally, perseverance upon the Tongariro will return a dividend sooner or later, but if our progress down her banks and through her many and varied pools has not proved too dull, it is my earnest wish that somewhere in the preceding chapters you have acquired a little more knowledge of her. She has so much to offer the angler in his quest for the elusive trout. She can be pliant and generous, temperamental or obstinate in her willingness to yield. There will be days when you will despair and conclude she is barren, and others when cast after cast produces a strike which chills yet excites the heart.

Of one thing, I am certain: the more time one spends with her, the more one studies her, contemplates her and, yes, I say it unashamedly, loves her, the greater are her rewards.

Perhaps one day we shall meet by one of her pools, for having found her I don't intend to leave her. She ranks as one of the great trout rivers of the world, and I count my blessings that I am privileged to live near her banks, lure a rainbow from her depths, and reveal her delights to others who, from far away, have come to make their pilgrimage.

Tongariro, this is my salute.

CHAPTER 10

THE DELTA

IT SEEMS A NATURAL PROGRESSION, having followed the Tongariro throughout her fishable length, to examine her as she meets Lake Taupo.

Befitting her stature, she differs from the other waterways which feed the lake and forms a delta, comprising four distinct fingers. Commencing from the southernmost they are, the Blind Mouth, the First Mouth, the Hook and the Main. The latter three are more than half a mile apart, with perhaps a quarter of a mile separating the Blind and the First.

I am hazarding a guess here, but I suggest that from these four mouths more fish are taken on a fly than in any other area of Lake Taupo. I have seen days, which Mr Hintz has described so well in *Trout at Taupo*, when everyone in the picket fence at Waitahanui is catching fish, and others when the Tauranga Taupo mouth has produced limits to every angler who can cast a fly. But the Tongariro Delta is supreme. It can play host to 30 boats spread among its mouths in holiday season, and few who persevere will return without success. Its advantages are obvious. With the Blind Mouth, which in fact offers a choice of two adjacent outlets, facing roughly south, the First looking west, the Hook offering a choice of two or three rips between north-west and south-west, and the Main, these last two years at any rate, having its outlet to the north-east, a selection may be made to avoid heavy wind from practically any quarter.

I realise I'm laying myself open to endless argument on the merits of each mouth, but I have a distinct preference to having the breeze at my back when fishing the Delta. Trout, I contend, favour a windward shore when all other factors, such as available food supply, are equal. Therefore, should the wind be from the west or south-west, my first anchorage will be at the Main Mouth which faces north-east. (I can visualise a few veterans remarking to themselves, "When the wind really decides to blow from the south-west or west in Turangi,

"They hogged the pool. I couldn't get a go at all," says Jim Stead (*left*). Bob, his brother and sister Marie Gilkison seem unrepentant.

you've got nowhere else to go." To these bearers of pearls of wisdom I doff my cap.) Conversely, on a north-easterly, my initial choices would be the Hook or the First.

There are a few pointers to a successful foray at the Delta which might be of use to the proud possessor of a new runabout. To a larger or lesser degree, the waters of the river cross an extensive shallow before dropping away over an extremely deep lip into the lake proper.

Varying from day to day, depending on wind and weather, it is possible to distinguish a flow of river water as it meets the lake and forms a distinct vee formation obvious on the surface. Trout have a preference, in the warmer months of the year, for the colder water supplied by the river, and the same apparently holds true for the smaller fish. Thus, where the feed fish are, there too, are the trout.

The object, then is to anchor your boat so that the stern is just overhanging the deep water, and if you're fortunate enough to have first option of a rip, as these vees are called, as nearly to the centre of it as is possible.

For the most part, fish are struck on or near to the bottom, and to this end it is necessary to wait for the line to sink completely before commencing a fairly slow retrieve. When guiding someone who has not fished the Delta previously I have a fairly set pattern of instruction. It does not vary much from, "Make your maximum length of cast, false cast or rail an additional ten to twenty feet which the current will pull out, commune with nature for a full minute or longer and then retrieve, a foot at a time and fairly slowly."

There are times when this pattern can be changed to advantage, especially when fish are smelting freely on the surface, but I remember the advice of an oldtimer, when trout were rising in great numbers at the Hatepe mouth one January.

"For every one you see on the surface, young fellow," he told me, "there must be twenty on the bottom."

Without doubt, in deep water such as the Delta provides, this counsel is worth noting.

"That's fine," you may remark, "but unless I'm waiting to start fishing at 4.55 am, I'm lucky at busy periods to have first choice of a rip." True enough. Let's then take a hypothetical case in which you have decided that the Hook offers the best opportunity to provide good sport. You arrive to find three boats already anchored in the rip you would like to fish. If you think as I do, you immediately swear twice under your breath and wonder how the deterioration in the country's economy can be balanced with the ever-increasing numbers of boat-owners.

Do not, however, despair and decide that a round of golf is the only solution. Faced with a situation such as this, my preference lies to the windward side of the assembled craft. Not only are you saved the tiring exercise of pushing line into wind, but the pull of the current appears much stronger from this quarter. I've selected this position on many occasions and been proved wrong, but on balance I'm sure that it is a safer bet than the other option.

The Delta fishes pretty well at any time of the year, but February, March, April and May provide some superlative catches of trout in prime condition. During these months they gather for the last ferocious gourmandising prior to their journeys upstream for the annual spawning, and fish hooked at this period are big, strong and spectacular to fight.

If they are in the mood, the selection of fly patterns is not much of a problem. Of course we all have our favourites, but generally the flies used extensively in the rivers do a good job at the mouth. My own selection favours the following:—

Boats fishing The Hook at the Tongariro Delta in the early morning.

Tongariro River and Delta showing (*left to right*) the Main Mouth, the Hook, the First Mouth and the Blind. The new tailrace from the Tokaanu Powerhouse is at right.

Daytime: Mrs Simpson, Red Setter, Rabbit and Yellow, Hammill's Killer, Hairy Dog, Partridge.
Night-time: Mrs Simpson, Hairy Dog, Craig's Night Time, Black Phantom, Scotch Poacher.

I have a preference for red bodies on most of these, and normally fish a little larger hook size than I do in the rivers: 4's, 6's and 8's should be included in your flybox with some of the night patterns extending to no. 2.

I know full well that half the readers of this book (even if they do number only five) will decide that my selection omits some proven killers of fish. Please accept my apology if you are a devoted user of a Dappled Dog with a yellow body or a green orbit tied on a 2/0.

That most flies will produce at some time or another at the Delta is not in dispute, and I had this brought home to me most forcibly when Lester Colby from Montana visited in November 1971. Mrs Colby has a wide reputation in the world of roses and had been invited to judge at the International Rose Show held, I think for the first time in New Zealand, at Hamilton. Lester was known to me before his arrival as an expert angler and I was looking forward with anticipation to the five days we should be spending together. He is welcome back any time he chooses to come, for not only was he a charming client and companion, but he taught me a tremendous amount of fishing lore, learned over the years in his home State.

Because so much of his fishing had been concerned with matching the hatch when casting to rising trout, he had become an ardent student of nature. For the uninitiated, matching the hatch refers to the practice of selecting a dry fly which so closely resembles the natural insect hatching at that time on stream or lake, as to be indistinguishable from the real thing to a selective trout. Lester tied practically all his own flies, exquisitely too, I must add, and although he had copied many New Zealand patterns before leaving home, he had also brought along some which he had used with success in the United States.

Fish were smelting quite freely around the Delta on the first day we visited it, but as is so often the case when this occurs, the trout were proving difficult in the extreme to take. There were no fewer than six boats working at the Hook and most had resigned themselves to a long, hard, and not particularly fruitful day.

Lester had invited me to fish and for more than an hour we

experimented with orthodox New Zealand smelt imitations. In all that time, despite evidence of an abundance of fish all around us, he hooked only one, and that a long skinny kelt which was so hungry it would have attacked an asparagus roll. Lester investigated his thirty or so flyboxes and finally produced something that resembled nothing I had seen before or since. Imagine, if you can, a feather lure only slightly smaller than an adult budgerigar, predominantly pale blue in colour, sporting a thinly tied silver tinsel body, the blue feather generously interspersed with white. The contraption was tied to an extremely long-shanked no. 4 hook.,

"How do you think this will go?" he wanted to know.

I gazed at the thing in awe. "Is it tame and housetrained?" I asked. "Frankly I think as soon as it hits the water every trout with a reasonably developed sense of self protection will head for the furthermost part of the lake."

He smiled his gentle smile. "Well, we're not exactly wearing our reels out while using your Kiwi specials," he said, "so why don't we have a crack with this?"

"You go right ahead," I told him, "but don't ask me to try and cast that thing. I've too much respect for my rod tip. Anyway, you do have a chance of getting a fish on it. If one rises as the fly hits the water, you'll probably stun it and we can pick it up in the net."

He tied the wierd thing on and began false casting. Each time it passed overhead there was a whirring sound not dissimilar to a helicopter warming up. It hit the water, floated for a moment until the feather became saturated and then, like a submerging submarine, slowly disappeared from view.

A couple of trout rose within feet of his line. "See," I said, "they're panic-stricken. Those will be the last ones in the queue for the mass migration to destinations unknown."

"How about pouring a cup of coffee while this thing sinks?" he asked, completely ignoring my pessimism.

"Sinks?" I said. "That thing will go down like a lead-filled hamburger."

Lester accepted his cup, took a sip, placed it on the seat beside him, and began his retrieve. One pull, a hesitation, a second pull and all hell broke loose. His rod top snapped down, his reel started to reverse at an alarming rate and the grin on his face was a thing of beauty.

"A fluke," I said. "The trout thought it was being attacked and had to defend itself in the only way it knew."

"You'll be begging for one of these in a few minutes," he laughed. "And after all the rudeness, you just might have to beg for a long time."

He brought a fine 4 lb maiden fish to my net and, like so many of his countrymen with conservation uppermost in their minds, gently removed the hook and slipped it back into its natural environment. (I wonder when New Zealanders who cannot possibly eat the catch of a successful day will follow the lead given to us and adopt the same policy? When, like in so many other parts of the world, it is too late?)

Lester made another cast, sipped his coffee, gave me a wink and again started to retrieve. It had happened again.

"Scares them away, does it?" he asked. "They're coming from miles away to try and get first crack at it."

I was beginning to believe it, too, but assured him that this one was undoubtedly foul-hooked in the tail as it tried to escape. We netted it, released it and he placed his box containing a dozen of the giant lures tantalisingly close to me.

"I'd hate to see a fellow like you reduced to begging," he said. "Help yourself."

"But it doesn't make any sense," I insisted. "Not one fly in the whole range of Taupo patterns has pale blue as a component. Browns, blacks, yellows, buffs, brindles, golds and greens, yes, and every combination you can think of. But no pale blue."

"Just look at what you've been missing all these years then," he said. "Go into business and you'll make a fortune."

I didn't let on that my fly tying was inexpert and, these days, infrequent. "Catch just one more in the next five minutes or so and I'll weaken," I said.

Something went wrong on his next cast, but on the following one he was again fast into a fish. I didn't wait until he had played it out. I grabbed that flybox, jettisoned my silver-bodied rabbit and tied on the latest discovery.

The next two days contributed more fish than two weeks of good, average fishing. Occasionally, convinced that there were so many fish in the area that any fly would take them, we would experiment. Immediately the action slowed or stopped completely. On went the Blue Budgie, as I now called it, and within a cast or two we were back in business.

Dr Ron Kennedy brought a friend out for the afternoon on the second day and dropped anchor alongside us. "How's the fishing?" he asked.

"Wonderful," we said. "We're almost tired of bringing them in."

Ron looked a little sceptical and proceeded to cast, as he can, half-way across the lake. It is not often that a double strike occurs, but Lester and I were each merrily playing a fish within seconds of each other. Ron's scepticism disappeared and, full of anticipation, he made his retrieve. Nothing. A dozen more casts and still his score was zero. I might mention here that if you can outfish the good Doctor you're doing pretty well or having a lucky streak.

"You'd better try one of Mr Colby's flies," I advised, passing one over. "They're the only thing we can take them on."

Ron looked incredulous, then aghast. "God!" he said, "What the devil is it?" But he tied it on.

He still talks about it to this day. "It was," he recalls, "like casting a live fantail but, oh dear, didn't it catch fish!"

Lester left me the balance of his collection when he reluctantly departed. They have been shared or lost, but I have already requested some more from him, and with the smelting season due in November if the shockingly low lake level permits any of the smelt hatch to survive, I'm eagerly searching each post for a small packet post-marked Missoula, Montana.

The Delta is, of course, reserved for fly fishing only within a radius of 300 yards of each mouth. Indeed, this restriction applies to all streams entering Lake Taupo. It is a good rule, for were it otherwise trollers and spin casters would take tremendous toll of the fish which seek their sustenance in the cold waters supplied by the rivers.

Trollers do, on occasions, take the risk and move in close to the rips of the Delta, but they risk confiscation of gear, a visit to the Magistrate's Court and the certain ire of legally-fishing fly casters moored at the mouth. What the erring ones do not appear to realise is that it is impossible to reel in 100 yards of lead-core line and proceed to the required distance should a ranger's boat appear. Most, when caught—and there are many prosecutions for the offence in any year—plead ignorance, but the stipulation is plainly evident on each and every fishing licence. I know many fishermen who have never read the numerous do's and don'ts on both the front and the reverse side of the licence but, as in all law, ignorance thereof is no excuse.

Chief Ranger or Chief Wildlife Officer as he is officially designated,

Trevor Thompson tells a lovely story concerning a troller and the 300-yard limit. Trevor was spending a quiet hour anchored at the Hook in an endeavour to pick up a couple of fish for friends one day when a small boat hove into view. Obviously it was trolling and just as obviously it was well within the stipulated minimum distance from the mouth. Its sole occupant appeared completely unconcerned at the gesticulations of occupants of other boats in the vicinity and proceeded to manoeuvre on a parallel almost within casting distance. This blatant disregard for legalities proved too much for Trevor and although on holiday, he emitted a gentle roar, at the same time producing his large and distinct notice which proclaims: "STOP. RANGER." The elderly troller looked up, peered shortsightedly and exclaimed "Danger? Danger? I don't see anything dangerous," and continued on his way. He got away with it too. Trevor was laughing too much to retrieve the anchor and give chase, and as he later remarked, if the old fellow was unable to read the sign from 30 yards it was obvious he could not decipher the regulations in small print on his licence. If, indeed, he had one.

There was one occasion when unwittingly flouting the 300-yard restriction paid off handsomely for a good friend of mine, Vic Rose. Vic had lived in Turangi for nearly three years before he allowed himself to be talked into the purchase of fishing tackle. His boat, a handsome thing with a big powerful outboard motor had been used by him and his wife Jill mainly for waterskiing. Vic arose bright and early one morning and expressed his intention of trying out his newly acquired trolling rod. Jill had no intention of accompanying him at that hour and went back to sleep.

We had already accepted an invitation to a convivial glass at the Rose's that evening and Vic told his story. "I didn't start trolling until I was nearly at the Delta," he said. "I let out about eighty yards of line and headed in towards a couple of anchored boats which were fishing. I thought that they couldn't possibly know less than I and if they thought there should be fish in that particular area, that was good enough for me. I got within about fifty yards of them when I had a strike. The fellows in the boats were very friendly and encouraging and kept waving to me while I played it toward the boat. Probably I did everything wrong, but at last I landed it."

Those of us present who were fisherfolk were trying to imagine how we should have reacted were we fly casting and a troller was poaching on our preserve.

"Did you happen to notice if the fly men were waving with closed fists?" someone wanted to know.

"I didn't really pay too much attention," said Vic, "but despite the wind I could hear them yelling a lot. Anyway, it was a big fish. Twelve pounds."

We guffawed, someone made the obvious observation that it is normal to remove the 10-pound bag of sugar from the kitchen scales before placing the fish thereon, and Vic was subjected to a barrage of barracking.

Jill finally made herself heard. "There's nothing wrong with my scales," she defended. "I saw the trout weighed and it was exactly twelve pounds."

Our hooting stopped. "Where was this monster?" we wanted to know. "Did he intend to have it mounted? Had the local weekly paper seen it and photographed it?"

"It's in the deep freeze," Vic said resignedly. "I didn't realise it was anything out of the ordinary. It's all cut up in steaks."

There was a mad rush to the kitchen, the freezer door was lifted and plastic bags of trout hastily emptied. Like a jigsaw puzzle we laid piece against piece, almost in reverence, until a giant body sans head, sans tail was assembled. We gazed in awe at the heaviest rainbow body we had seen for some years and slowly turned to face a crest-fallen Vic.

"Almost every fisherman I know," someone said, "would have had this magnificent specimen mounted in a place of honour. In future years his grandchildren will have forgotten his golf handicap, his success in the business world, even an odd Victoria Cross or two, but never could they fail to honour a man who had caught a trout such as this."

Vic took a long pull at his gin and tonic. "Never mind," he said "with my luck I'll get another tomorrow."

We looked at him pityingly and decided he should be taught some facts of life. "Not only will you probably never catch another within four pounds of that," we said "but you were trolling illegally. You were fortunate not to have been apprehended by a ranger, who not only would have demanded to see your licence, but in all likelihood would have confiscated not only your fish but your new rod to boot."

Vic was quite unabashed. "He couldn't have done that," he said.

"Why?" we asked. "You can't refuse. It merely compounds the offence. You'd be in worse trouble once you got to Court."

"Oh, no. He couldn't have done that," Vic insisted. "You see, I'd forgotten to buy a licence, so how could I produce one?"

It was quite a party that night.

Should the fishing be slow at the Delta, it is often pleasant to beach the boat and to wander quietly up the banks of the Tongariro. In these shallow lower reaches fish lie in numbers but, as I remarked earlier when discussing Bayard Fox's escapade, they are difficult in the extreme to take during daylight hours. The more impressive species here are the browns. Coming up behind them as one does when walking upstream, it is possible to station oneself within a couple of feet of them as they lie quietly basking in the willow filtered sunshine.

Some of them are genuinely enormous, and one I saw a couple of years ago gave me the urge to do battle with it. It was the sole occupant of a narrow stretch of water about 50 yards up from the Blind mouth, and was obviously ruler of his kingdom. Let another fish venture too close and the big fellow was immediately on the warpath. It is nearly impossible to estimate the weight of a fish which is lying in 2 or 3 feet of water, but this old cannibal made respectable 6- and 8-pounders of his own breed look like fry.

I was more enthusiastic on night fishing then than I am now (although a balmy evening can still be wonderfully pleasant and can still tempt me out), and I made my preparations with patience. This fish, I was certain, would scale in excess of 16 lb and might even make 20. He had not grown to this size and age by living a life of recklessness and blind adventure.

I calculated that I should have to wait for at least a week before making my play, for the moon was nearly full and I felt that darkness would prove an ally. On almost every one of those seven evenings I crept upstream from the Blind Mouth like an Indian scout, fearful that he would have disappeared. It was January, and boats and vacationing picnickers were swarming around the Delta. What if he had gone? What if someone else had discovered him and had already sent him to a taxidermist for mounting? Always, however, he remained in his pool, lord and master of all he surveyed. What a fight I should have on my hands if only I could induce him to strike.

A Monday evening provided the perfect conditions, so my diary tells me. It also states "stalked big brown at Blind Mouth. Struck on fourth cast of Craig's Night Time, tied on no. 4 hook. Broken leader in about 2 seconds flat," which is a pretty bald statement for an experience which left my heart in a fierce spasm of palpitation and the hair on the back of my neck horizontal.

It says nothing of the patient wait beside the beached boat, of the prayers that the cloud would not clear from the waning moon, of the stealthy approach to the one position above my fish which I had estimated would leave my backcast free of the overhanging willows. It does not recall the slow, silent slippery entrance into water which was suprisingly and alarmingly deep, nor does it note how even the sound of my reel, as I carefully removed exactly 14 yards of line, put my teeth on edge.

I had selected an 8-foot fibre glass rod for the job; not because I should not have preferred something with more power, but because I calculated that my normal 9-footers just might allow my fly to finish high in a tree behind me. A sinking-tip line would, I estimated, get the fly sufficiently far under the surface to save my giant the necessity of rising for the lure. Although I had stepped off the distance from where I now stood to his favourite lie half a dozen times, and knew it to be 42 feet, I was still worried that on his nightly peregrination he might have moved far downstream or—perish the thought—already have been terrorised as I entered the water.

My leader had been carefully tied in a series of tapers from a 20lb test down to 7lb at the tippet. I should have liked more, but the name of the game was, firstly, to hook the fish and then start worrying. Too heavy a leader and, despite the dark, he might ignore the lure. Each blood knot had been checked and rechecked.

I started to false cast, worrying all the time about the trees at my back, but my survey had been good and the line shot out about 30 feet. I had decided to start short, as I do habitually, and increase distance with each successive throw.

There is something eerie and uncanny about fishing on a night when the moon is hidden and you are far removed from the normal sounds of habitation. Uncanny, yes, but beautiful too. The sound of birds disturbed from sleep by even your quietest approach is distinct, and even here, where the river moves serenely and quietly on its path, the whirls and eddies of the current are heard with a clarity not encountered during daylight hours.

At night the rod feels longer, less manageable, the invisible line could be bowing unseen, presenting difficulties should a strike occur. One's usually sensitive fingers explore the coils like a cluster of uneducated thumbs. You wait, scarcely daring to breathe.

Another cast, adding a few more feet, successfully achieved. It must have been more into the current for I felt the drag on the line and hastily mended it back upstream. It swung to my side of the river and I started a slow retrieve. Nothing. Cast three, I estimated, should be close to him, if he were still in his chosen haunt, but once again there was no hesitation in the free path of the swinging line.

I released the last few coils, false cast, and felt the satisfying smack against the reel which indicates that more line could have been cast had it been required. Once again, I mended upstream, the line swung, I waited a moment longer and began the retrieve. One pull of a foot, another, yet another with no check, and then I had him.

Browns are not hurried in their strike as a rule, but I had expected something different from this cousin of the Loch Ness Monster. I had visualised an enormous pull at the rod tip, a frantic flapping in the blackness of the water below me, a strike worthy of the grand proportions of the fish. The fly merely stopped. Was I snagged? Slowly my reel turned a couple of times on the spool. It was no snag. I struck, and for good measure, struck again. There was one angry shake of a huge body and the sickening realisation that the rod was now vertical, unstrained, defeated. I reeled in, groped for my leader and ran my shaking fingers down its length. One, two, three blood knots and then . . . nothing. Uncaring now, I switched on my pocket torch. It was all too obvious. The last 15 inches of leader had been broken with only a minimum of effort by my brownie. Yes, he'd become mine personally over the past week and already I was swearing a vendetta. Despite all my care, despite the preparations, he had won the first battle by a knockout in Round One.

I didn't rush back on the following evening, nor the next, but on the third day I again reconnoitred the river. For a few minutes I could not find him, but then from beneath the undercut bank of his home he appeared briefly. Again I saw the enormous tail, the breadth of back, the unbelievable depth and length of him and promised him aloud that his days were numbered.

A week after the first attempt I was back, but despite two hours of casting not a touch rewarded me throughout the evening. I tried again the next night, with the same result. I rested the pool for three more nights and made what was to prove my last foray.

Pitch-black, a suggestion of rain in the air, windless. Perfect. The same equipment but now a 12 lb tippet. Let him try and break that.

I'd never fished for trout with such a hawser in my life. It would, I was sure, handle a mako shark if necessary.

Again I beached the boat and made the same circuitous route to my casting position. Again I slipped quietly down the bank into the inky water and again I started with the short cast. One throw, two, ten, twenty casts and I was becoming resigned to another fruitless night. "He's learned his lesson," I thought. "I'll give him another couple with the Craig's Night Time and then try a Hairy Dog or a Black Phantom."

By now I had the technique of casting from the position to a fine art and the encroaching willows were no problem. Stripping off another 3 feet of line, I shot the cast across and down, felt the drag as the current grabbed it, mended once and then again. It was still swinging when I felt it stop. Almost by instinct I struck, not fiercely but positively and felt the solid, spine-tingling weight of my fish. For a moment there was a stalemate. I could imagine him lying there, disbelieving that he could have made a second mistake within a week. Then slowly, with awful strength he turned and moved downstream. Not for him the mad, panic-stricken flight of a rainbow. Unhurriedly he pulled off 10 yards of line and I remember thinking that he was just too confident for my wellbeing. It was too early yet to make my play and we settled to a long tug-of-war. I was cursing the dark, cursing the steep 3-foot bank I should have to negotiate if I were to land him, cursing my lack of foresight in omitting to bring a net. There were a couple of places to beach him, but how would I find them in the dark?

He was by far the heaviest trout I had ever tried to handle. Back in 1955 I had fought and won a 25-minute struggle with a 19¼-pounder in Lake Tarawera, but this fellow, I was sure now, was the greater fish. Ten minutes elapsed. He for his part was in no hurry. I, for mine, was perspiring freely. He gained a few yards. I wound a few back. Five more minutes and still no advantage was gained on either side.

"He must start to tire soon," I thought, "but I can't use any more pressure."

Once more my reel began to give line, but this time it did not stop after a couple of yards. Without haste, but still with impressive power he forged his way downstream. Ten yards lost, twenty, my nervous fingers telling me that by now I was deep into the backing. I tried a little more strain through the rod. It had as much effect as halting a departing liner with a farewell streamer.

It was time to climb the bank and follow. Rod held aloft, I grasped a treetrunk with my left hand and hoisted myself into a sitting position on the edge. I continued to lose line. Saplings stung my face as I struggled to my feet, tree roots seemed determined to trip me. Almost in panic I floundered through the darkness, reeling, reeling all the time. He stopped. *Whew*! I could feel the casting line returning to the reel; how much I could not calculate. The weight returned to the rod tip and I stopped. God! Wouldn't he ever realise he was beaten?

It was a couple of minutes before I realised something was wrong with the fight. No trout lies completely still for that length of time. There is, at least, a lateral movement, but this fellow had not changed position at all. An odd twitch through the length of the rod down into my hand assured me he was still attached, but something was terribly, dreadfully wrong. Reluctantly, awkwardly, I groped with my left hand for the torch. I followed the beam from the tip of the rod, down the length of line to the water. I nearly wept. No more than twelve yards from shore, a clump of willow, perhaps 6 feet in diameter and 4 feet long had long ago become firmly embedded in the sandy bottom. Not even the leader was showing where the line entered it on the up-river side. I tried more pressure, then desisted as I sensed the breaking point.

There was, I decided, only one solution. Somehow I must work my way out to the snag and try and ease him back through his entry point, by hand if necessary. One thing was certain. He would not return the way he had come of his own volition. I had one factor in my favour: the water here was shallow, no deeper than 3 feet as I remembered it. Once more I slid down the bank, nearly fell as my boot became entangled in a submerged root, righted myself and began to take in line as I moved out into the stream. An occasional bump through the rod reassured me. At least he was still there. Painfully slowly I reached the head of the snag, and with heart in mouth released enough slack to reach the line with my left hand. Gingerly I followed it down. Where the hell was the leader? Forget the wet sleeve as I explored deeper. At last the greasy touch I was searching for. Deeper with the arm. Dear Lord, why hadn't I brought a net? "Idiot," I kept repeating to myself. By the length of leader I guessed he was nearly to the downstream side of the obstruction. It was just possible he would have remained sufficiently quiet for me to have netted him from behind. Would he, though, fit into a standard net?

I tightened on the leader and gained a foot. Something rebelled on the other end and I let go hastily. I had lost perhaps two feet and, grope as deeply as I could, my hand met only casting line. This could go on for ever, or more likely with no real pressure on him, he would decide on another effort to free himself of the fly.

Gently I started to pull. One foot. Two, three. I could grasp the leader now. Bless him, he was coming through. Softly now. Even an inch gained was a major breakthrough. Another foot, and then it stopped solid. Man does some crazy things at times of great stress. It was at this moment, that in desperation, I committed the greatest error of judgement of my piscatorial career. To this day I shudder when I think of it. Frantic, I switched on the torch, played it down the leader, saw where it was draped over one small twig and saw my fish. For perhaps two seconds there was no reaction from him, and then, still not at great speed, he half turned, gave a beat or two of that mighty tail and with almost disdainful ease, broke the leader.

"The one that got away" has always been, and will always be, the greatest fish one has ever hooked. Although some of the stories have to be taken with the proverbial grain of salt, it is likely that many of them are true, for the obvious reason that the stronger the fish the more chance he has to make good his escape. Certainly, this fellow was just too much trout for me to handle, especially in the dark. He called the tune and I was the one to dance.

Did I try for him again? I was busy with clients for a couple of weeks after the episode, but I did have time during daylight hours to search for him in his adopted pool. He was not there. Nor have I seen him since. His lie has been occupied by other lesser browns, sometimes three or four at a time. He cannot be anywhere in the vicinity. He would never have permitted the intrusion.

You will, I feel sure, enjoy your fishing from the Delta. A fish hooked in comparatively still and deep water is not as spectacular in its antics nor in its fight as if it were taken in the river, but during the hot months when the streams are either barren or playing host to a preponderance of kelts (or slabs or spawn-outs as they are also known) the Delta can offer excellent sport.

One word of warning when discussing the Delta: you are perhaps wondering, if you do not possess a boat, whether it is fishable by wading. Under certain circumstances and in some places only, it is.

To reach it by car, it is necessary to travel down Grace Road to the end. A gate which is unlocked will allow you entrance to Fearon Grace's property. Follow the well defined though bumpy road to his house—not the first one you come to, which is uninhabited—and ask permission to proceed. This will be readily given upon access payment of a dollar per car. The track can then be followed to within a couple of hundred yards of the Main Mouth. Should a few boats be fishing here, you would do better to proceed on foot around the beach to the Hook, for the boats at the Main will be anchored well beyond the point where the tops of your waders will permit you to join them.

The Hook, the First and the Blind Mouth, however, can all be waded with care, providing—and I cannot emphasise this too strongly—the day is sunny and the water from the Tongariro is clear. It is vital that the lip where river meets lake is easily discernible, for the first false step in body waders could well be your last. Even when conditions such as these prevail, it is unwise in the extreme to venture closer than a rod's length from the edge, for the sandy bottom is inclined to be unstable and shifting.

Taking everything into consideration, it is a safer bet in all ways to make friends with someone who owns a boat. Even if you don't like him particularly!

CHAPTER 11

THE GENTLE ONES

TUMBLING FROM THE EASTERN MOUNTAINS to their final blending with the Lake come the delightful smaller streams and rivers. Alternately bubbling and serene, busy and indolent, boisterous and placid, they are separated at some points of their respective paths by only a few miles. Each, though, has its own charm, its own personality, its own secret places where trout rest before moving onward to the remembered spawning grounds. The Waitahanui, the Hinemaiaia (sometimes called the Hatepe), the Tauranga-Taupo, the Waimarino, the Waiotaka—names to bring nostalgia and longing to those who are separated from them, names made famous by the quality of the angling they offer, the delights they never fail to provide.

In places only a few feet in width, at others spreading wide and shallow to 40 yards, they harbour the pebbles and the necessary cover which provide ideal hatching grounds for the prospective spawners.

No purposeful, plunging power such as the Tongariro boasts here, no heavy, white, awesome current, no strength-sapping, careful, nervous wading, but streams to which we may return as we grow old or less sure or more frail or more content to dream, sure in the knowledge that we need not fear them nor our own infirmities.

Chuckling glides and runs and shallows proceed to slow limpid pools, deceptive in depth by their unparalleled clarity, where every stone shows bright and bold, where each trout can be discerned by the naked eye.

Pools, often only 10 feet in diameter and no more in length will, in the height of the day play host to 20 or more trout, lazily maintaining only sufficient momentum to hold station. Yet herein lies the challenge for, come upon them unexpectedly, suddenly, and the same placid pool becomes a seething mass of churning fish, totally unprepared to accept any offering for several hours to come. Stalk

Map of Lake Taupo showing principal streams and rivers which enter it. The lake itself is 26 miles long and 17 miles wide at its widest point and has an overall area of 238 square miles.

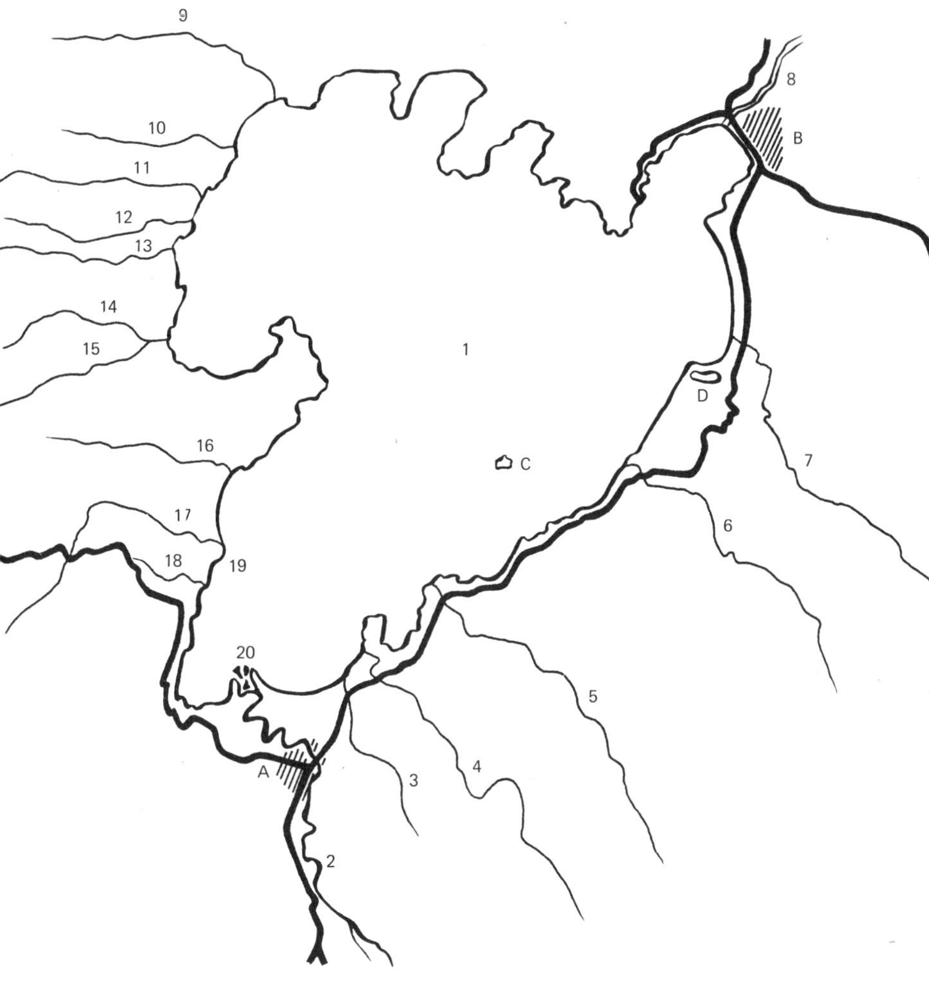

1. Lake Taupo
2. Tongariro River
3. Waiotaka Stream
4. Waimarino Stream
5. Tauranga Taupo River
6. Hatepe (Hinemaiaia) Stream
7. Waitahanui River
8. Waikato River
9. Waihora Stream
10. Otupoto Stream
11. Waihaha Stream
12. Otaunga Stream
13. Oruapuraho Stream
14. Whanganui Stream
15. Mangakara Stream
16. Whareroa Stream
17. Kuratau Stream
18. Omori Stream
19. Sandspit
20. Tongariro River Delta

A. Turangi
B. Taupo
C. Motutaiko Island
D. Lake Rotongaio

Left: The author's wife, Josephine, throws an educated line downstream on the Cliff reach of the Waiotaka Stream and . . . *Right:* . . . reverts to her favourite technique, nymphing, on one of the Top Camp pools.

them, however, with patience and skill—false casting with line in the air at all times until the presentation is exact—and the rewards can be wonderful.

To follow each stream pool by pool as we have followed the Tongariro would be tedious for the reader, possibly more so for the writer and would serve no really useful purpose, for the pools on all, with the possible exception of part of the Waitahanui, are obvious. A pool, a glide, a shallow, a pool is the pattern, as it is upon most of our North Island rivers, and the beginner will recognise the holding water as surely as the man of experience.

It is the way in which they are fished which is most important, and in these little streams knowhow will pay a dividend. In downstream angling with a wet fly or lure the first rule to be observed is to remain well back from the pool which you intend to fish. Surely it's nice to know that the particular hole you are about to cast into has fish in it, but go up close to it, peer into it, and you have just made the next hour or so a waste of time. There is a saying with which I concur—if you can see the trout from an upstream position, the trout can also see you. It is probable, especially when the water is gin-clear and the day bright, that the fish will be in the deepest part of the pool. Useless then to toss a fly with a splash right on top of the trout. Try to make your presentation to the shallow side of the holding water and let the fly swing to the side of the stream where the trout are congregated. Often this is impossible or impractical because of overhanging bush or trees, and it is infinitely more desirable at such times to land the fly in the riffle leading into the head of the pool and pay off line until the lure is where you guess the trout to be.

That trout have quite remarkable upward vision I have not the slightest doubt, for many times I have crept Red Indian style to the top of a bank overhanging a pool, raised my head a fraction to obtain visibility and seen fish swirl and dart in alarm.

If you wish to satisfy yourself that fish are indeed in a likely looking hole there is one way and one way only in which they can be approached, and then with infinite care, and that is from behind. Polarised glasses are the next-best thing to essential, for the removal of glare from the water will enable you to spot your fish from a far greater distance than you can achieve without them.

There are moments in one's angling life which lead to great elation coupled with anxiety. The first, and almost certainly my own favourite, is fighting a fish in fast, heavy water. Will she, now so near to the tail of the pool, decide that her final means of salvation is to slip over the brink into the tumbling rapids below? Will she find some hidden snag and take refuge behind it, drawing the tippet of your leader among the projecting twigs until the strain proves too much and she goes on her way rejoicing? Will she suddenly turn back upstream with the pace of a startled cougar, gaining sufficient slack line to throw the hook? These and a dozen other questions flash through one's mind while the battle is being won or lost, and no matter how many fish one catches during a lifetime, they still insinuate themselves.

On small streams such as the Waiotaka and Waimarino, the worries are different, but they are still uppermost in one's mind. With only a tiny pool in which to make her attempt to escape, it is unlikely that she is going to remain in the immediate vicinity for very long. Almost inevitably she turns downstream, rushes through the shallows, throwing spray to left and right, and the consternation starts at that moment. Will she wrap the leader around those exposed stones in her hectic flight? Will she dive under that overhanging blackberry bush with its trailing thorny branches hanging low into the water? If she descends to the pool below to continue the fight, is that manuka branch still lying across the better part of half the hole? Furthermore, in order to improve one's chance of a strike, it is probable that the tippet size has been reduced, and, with fish of the same weight as one encounters in the Tongariro, the odds on a broken leader are fairly high.

And yet aren't these worries what fishing is all about? If we won all our battles, would we still want to go fishing? More often than not, the memory of the trout lost after a thrilling fight remains with us much longer than the one we beach or net successfully. As a golfer I know full well that if I had shot a 66 every time I visited the course I would have tossed the game away. No longer would the challenge have been there. Thus would it be were we to land every fish.

The Waiotaka

Starting from Turangi, the first stream one encounters along the eastern shore towards Taupo is the Waiotaka. At the bridge on No. 1 Highway, it resembles little more than a 10-foot-wide ditch carrying clear water gently down to the lake. Surely not a stretch upon which to waste time with rod and reel, the stranger might think, and how mistaken he would be. High fescue grass and blackberry surmount the banks both upstream and down, but the lazily moving Waiotaka will provide fishing thrills aplenty if you approached it in the manner of a stalker of wild game. Let the natural cover work for you where you can, rather than rebel and curse against it, for the fish are alert to clumsy movement. If necessary, make your cast on hands and knees to remain clear of their ever watchful gaze.

There are a couple of miles of fishable water from the main highway downstream and a little more on the upstream side of the bridge, but much of the latter is nearly unfishable because of dense overhanging willows which frame the river in a green arch, making casting difficult in the extreme.

From the old Korohe ford upstream the Hautu Prison Farm borders both banks of the Waiotaka and permission is necessary before making access.

Undoubtedly, except when the waters of this superb stream are discoloured by recent rains, the Waiotaka provides its bounty more readily to the exponent of nymph fishing than to any other method. It is also a type of angling to which I have become progressively more attached, and on the Waiotaka as well as the Waimarino and Tauranga-Taupo I follow it as often as I can.

Nymphing upstream and across is as near as we can get in these rivers of the Taupo basin to the thrills the dry fly has to offer. It certainly lacks the precision of the best of dry fly expertise, but at least one is fishing to trout which can be seen from behind and that is thrill enough at any time.

Family business.
Bruce Steward, the author's brother-in-law, nymphs the Waiotaka.

Either a floating line or one of the new wet-tip variety can be used when nymphing and my own choice, as explained earlier, inclines to the wet-tip. The object of the exercise is to present the nymph far enough above the trout to enable it to sink by the time it has reached the fish. Generally the quarry will be lying in the deep part of the pool and favouring the bank on that side. The approach is thus made from the downstream, shallow side and the cast made upstream and across. The line is retrieved at sufficient pace to allow the nymph to float freely through the current and toward the trout. To achieve this natural motion a slight belly must be maintained in the line, for without it the nymph will be pulled through the lie instead of tumbling on every whim of the current. To a trout, it just will not look like the natural you wish to represent.

There are several good nymphs available from tackle stores, but of them all my preference lies to a bright-orange body dressed only with sparse hackle and tail and tied on a no. 12 or no. 14 hook. I like too, to utilise a tapered leader to a 3 x tippet and not less than 9 feet in length, and sometimes when the water is extremely low and clear this is increased to 12 feet.

Probably no other factor is more important when nymphing than concentration. It is rarely that one feels the strike as a fish hits, for the slack in the line does not allow the shock to be transmitted to the rod tip and, as the dry fly man must constantly watch his fly bobbing downstream toward him, so the nymphing angler must not let his gaze waver from the end of his line. The nymph itself, of course, is invisible under water and so often the only means of determining a strike is to see the slight hesitation of the line tip as it moves downstream. It is imperative at this moment to lift the rod tip and remove the slack. Leave it one second too long and the fish will have decided that the nymph is inedible and will have rejected it.

Half a day of this type of fishing is fairly exhausting, as during that time my guess is that you will make about ten or a dozen times as many casts as you would were you wet fly fishing downstream. That it is, however, effective can be best borne out by the results my friends Jack Costello of Tauranga and Fred Goddard, whom you have already met in previous pages, obtained when we fished together on a glorious day in May. Our total in 5 hours was 34 fish actually landed and probably half as many lost either on the strike or during the fight. It's not always like that, but for my money, given good clear water conditions, the nymph will produce three or four trout to the wet fly's one in the small streams.

There will be days, of course, when heavy falls of rain have discoloured the water to a marked degree and the stream is running higher than normal. These conditions are ideal for downstream fishing and, providing the water is not completely muddy in ap-

Four of the Waiotaka's regulars: Peter Wallis, "Carrots" Kennedy, Jack Costello and Ron Kennedy tell their lies over lunch.

pearance and consequently unfishable, will provide excellent sport. Gone is the fear of being seen by the trout if one ventures too close, and the cast may be made without the fish becoming line-shy. Remember too that during a rise in the river, the fish are likely to be holding in shallower water than is normal. Because they were not there just the other day when you could see every stone in the bottom, it doesn't mean that they're not there today when the stream is cloudy.

Let's emphasise it once again—fish all the water.

The Waimarino

The Waimarino is similar in many respects to the Waiotaka, and can be worked in the same manner, with either nymph or lure. Indeed, it has a couple of advantages. Its ease of access provides many miles of superb fishing with easy wading and, unlike the Waiotaka, no special permission is necessary in order to work the upper reaches.

Korohe Road runs off Highway 1 about five miles north of Turangi. Roughly a mile along this gravelled surface and one reaches a T formation, the left branch giving access to the lower pools and the right continuing for several miles upstream. As with the Waiotaka above the old ford, so are the upstream pools of the Waimarino above Korohe Pa closed for the months between 1 June and 30 November each year.

Especially during April and May however, it is to the upstream pools that I prefer to make my way. Generally, they are less inhabited than the lower reaches and the Waimarino itself has more character the further up one moves.

Above the bridge which crosses the narrow, deep gorge there are a couple of miles of the most attractive water one could wish to find anywhere. The best holding pools are fairly widely spaced and for this reason the stream has to be crossed and recrossed several times on the way upstream. However, rarely is the Waimarino sufficiently boisterous to make the journey difficult or hazardous, and there are many delights in the scenery which surrounds one.

By expressing a preference for the upper reaches, I do not wish to detract from the lower areas, for there are many thoroughly delightful and prolific pools here also. Any of four or five car tracks leaving the road on your left will take you close to the stream and, until one knows a river so thoroughly that it holds few surprises, there is

A typical stretch of the Waimarino Stream. The author tosses a nymph towards a natural lie.

always the anticipated thrill of the very next pool around the very next corner yielding the trout which will occupy the place of honour over the fireplace.

The Tauranga-Taupo

There are anglers who visit Lake Taupo year after year from comparative youth to near-senility who, for preference, fish no other water than the Tauranga-Taupo. They fall in love at the impressionable age, marry her and remain enchanted, faithful and adoring until the end. They take no other mistress. To them the Tauranga-Taupo is synonymous with Taupo fishing. Their choice is not hard to understand, for she has her own particular charm as she meanders her leisurely way to her meeting with the lake.

Wider, less boisterous, deeper in many parts than the Waimarino, she offers good and often excellent fishing to both the lure and the nymph, the latter, naturally enough, producing the better in the glides and shallower pools where it can be sunk sufficiently quickly.

If you are new to the area, drive north approximately 8 miles from Turangi and 100 yards or so over the bridge which crosses the river you will see a sign which states categorically "No Admittance". Ignore it and drive through, circumnavigate an extensive quarrying undertaking and once past it, follow one of a dozen easily-negotiated car tracks which will lead you eventually to the river.

There is no particular stretch on these lovely waters which impresses me more than any other. Whether I am casting in the Maungakowhitiwhiti Pool or the Cliff, down the Avenue or the Parade, I am equally content. There is a peace, a serenity about the Tauranga-Taupo which in some inexplicable way transfers itself to the angler, so that if he returns emptyhanded, there's the feeling of "What the hell? It was just wonderful to be up there anyway."

One peculiar pattern does emerge with this river though, which I have not encountered elsewhere, certainly not to any marked degree anyway. On the Tauranga-Taupo I'm either as busy as a bee with his proverbial burden or casting with a feeling of hopelessness. Either the strikes and the action are fast and frequent—or all the effort produces a zero, a blank, a comprehensive skunking. Either the trout are barging each other aside to get at the fly or they are avoiding it like the plague, or whatever the piscatorial equivalent may be.

I had a friend over from Australia last year who was determined to fish every river flowing into Lake Taupo in one week flat. Of all the places to start, he elected the picket fence at Waitahanui which had intrigued him as he drove down to Turangi from the airport. I recall that our rods made the total 23, shoulder to shoulder spread out through the width of the rip in the gathering dusk. However, though I loathe fishing in the midst of a football scrum like that, Jim was determined to sample the lot. We plunged in to the plimsoll line and commenced flogging away. Jim, I recall, might have had the very edge of the current; I was so far removed from the centre of activity that I might as well have been casting from the beach. Those who had appeared at the first light of dawn and were consequently in the centre of the rip were taking the odd fish or two but I was certain that we were only getting Jim's casting arm going for future days ahead.

Dusk became dark. A sickle moon shed no light. Another hour and I'd had more than enough. "I'm going in," I told Jim but, mindful that he was on his first good vacation in four years added, "but you stay as long as you want."

I was reeling in as I started to move off when I felt the tug of a fish. At that identical moment, Jim hollered, "Got one!"

"Too much of a coincidence," I thought, "We've hooked the same trout and one of us hasn't got it in the mouth."

At that moment, I heard mine leave the water quite close inshore, while Jim's was becoming airborne in the opposite direction. Certainly, it was a genuine double strike. I was much more concerned that he get his first New Zealand trout than that I beach mine, so I stayed close to render such advice as might be helpful. His fish was being singularly uncooperative. Unlike the majority of trout hooked in a fairly fast water, which will turn downstream letting the current assist them, this fish should have been disqualified for foul play. It was moving parallel to the line of fishermen, broaching like a dolphin, and from the language heard through the inky night, was causing no end of bother to other anglers. Back it came on the same flight-path as Jim applied a bit of pressure, but still spending as much time out of the water as it did in it. If possible, the swearing was even more profane as angler after angler felt his line gathered up in Jim's.

"Get the — thing in," someone called from 30 yards or so away. "You've got my line all fouled up."

Naturally I couldn't see Jim's face but I gathered he must have been a little red around the gills by this time.

My own fish was pretty well beaten by then, but I let it lie quietly enough 20 feet or so from me, certain that I should be needed to disentangle half a dozen lines before Jim could land his precious trout. Off it went again, this time in the direction of Huka Falls about 9 miles distant, and from some four reels came the screaming that would normally bring a song of joy to the lips. The profanity would have gladdened the heart of a collector of pornography.

"Break it off," someone who was close to hysteria suggested.

Jim had remained quiet throughout, but the thought of sacrificing his hard-earned fish by deliberately stretching the leader past the breaking strain was too much for his good Australian blood to bear. "Go to hell" he drawled quietly but distinctly. "If you bastards think I've come twelve hundred bloody miles to break off my first fish, you must be crazy."

"O Gawd, A bloomin' Aussie," someone said, "I might have guessed it. Why don't you stay home and try and breed a Melbourne Cup winner?"

"Impossible," another voice spoke up, "they're even worse at that than they are at catching trout."

Jim, meantime, had turned the fish and was steadily gaining line.

"It won't be long now," I thought, "and then we can see how bad the tangle really is."

Suddenly there was a muffled Australian oath and Jim said "He's gone." What else can one say in such circumstances but "Bad luck"?

I began to tow my placid fish to shore while Jim prepared to cast again. I was half way in when I heard him utter a cry of complete distress and anger.

"Somebody's cut my line" he called, incredulous. It was all too true. Someone down the line had been so impatient, so callous, as to take a knife or a pair of scissors to Jim's new line. Fully 25 feet of it had gone with the fish, including the weight-forward taper of course.

It was a quiet ride back to Turangi, and apart from an odd muttered "Heathens!" and "Call themselves bloody sportsmen", Jim was too dejected, too bewildered to offer more than an odd monosyllabic reply to my attempts to cheer him up.

"Never mind," I said finally, "we'll try the Tauranga-Taupo tomorrow and see if our luck changes." Which brings me back, rather circuitously it is true, to the vagaries of this stream.

Jim's luck the next day more than compensated for his distressing

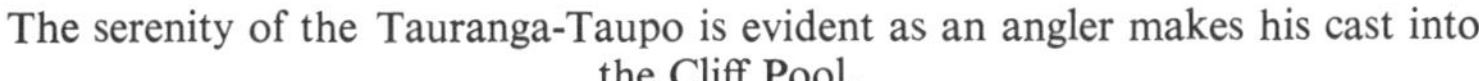

The serenity of the Tauranga-Taupo is evident as an angler makes his cast into the Cliff Pool.

The call of the stream is a strong call. Angler wastes no time on car doors before starting to fish the Tauranga-Taupo.

Pool, reach and rapid. Water to make a fisherman's heart beat faster. The Tauranga-Taupo on a perfect day.

experience at the picket fence. Fishing the Crescent he took a limit of 10 fish weighing 57 pounds. We had them smoked to his own recipe—manuka sawdust, to which every few hours he added green lemon leaves. A gourmet's delight, as so many of his friends in Melbourne verified.

With a day like that behind him Jim had changed his mind about fishing every stream in the basin. Back to the Tauranga-Taupo we headed early next morning, our high spirits matched only by our smug confidence in the sport which awaited us. The Crescent held no other rod and Jim moved in. I could feel the expectancy and excitement in the man. I smoked a cigarette for a while until he had a 40-yard start on me and then waded out and began casting. Two hours later we compared notes. Not a touch on either rod.

"They've moved on," I said "and there's been no run to replace them. Let's move upstream two or three miles and see if we can catch up with them." Throughout the rest of the day we fished that river as thoroughly as we knew how. We changed flies until every pattern had been introduced to the water. We changed to floating lines and nymphed upstream. Jim tried both New Zealand and Australian dry flies. We exchanged ideas with a dozen other disgruntled anglers. All to no avail. Overnight, affluence had become abject poverty.

So often this seems to be the pattern of the Tauranga-Taupo. Strike it as we did on that first day and she is more generous than any river in the area. Find her in another mood, however, and her handbag is not only shut but padlocked. And she has thrown away the key.

The Hinemaiaia (*Hatepe*).

Rushing from the artificial dams further up in the hills this delightful scenic valley stream can and does provide excellent fishing through March, April and May. Because the river falls rapidly, the pools are less clearly defined than on the others we have followed and a certain amount of local knowledge, coupled with trial and error methods will be necessary before the stable lies are found. It is not a stream I fish a lot, nor as much as I should like to, for there is so much good water closer to home and time spent on the road is fishing time wasted. However, it is seldom that I have returned from it empty handed, although reference to my diary tells me that currently I am landing only 50 per cent of the fish I have hooked in it. That's a poor return in anyone's language and is, I think, attributable

The lovely Hatepe Stream with Lake Taupo and Motutaiko Island in the distance.

to the fact that in many places the speed of the current is such that one is unable to follow the fish if it decides to head off downstream. Even if the trout is eventually turned, the long haul back up the fast-flowing eye of the current is often difficult enough to allow the hook to pull free.

Some of the pools, especially those immediately upstream from the No. 1 Highway bridge are easily discerned and not particularly difficult to fish, and as for the waters farther upstream, remember the adage that trout like depth combined with a flow of water which allows them to lie without being forced to continually fight the current. Mr Bruno Kemball of the Red Spinner Tackle Shop adjacent to the main highway at Hatepe always seems to know when a run has moved upstream, and is generous with advice on the methods and the tackle necessary to make your expedition fruitful.

The Waitahanui

To a vast number of anglers, Waitahanui is synonymous with fishing at Taupo. To many there is no other area worthy of consideration when making plans for the next excursion. Taupo, to them, is Waitahanui and Waitahanui is Taupo.

To the remainder of us it is a stream to which those who like it are welcome, for it plays host to more rods per mile than there are battens on a farm fence. Certainly there is no other district in New Zealand which offers such gregarious fishing. Hook a trout anywhere within view of the Number One Highway and you are guaranteed an audience which would flatter an entertainer of international reputation.

The "bush telegraph", that strange phenomenon which informs anglers from miles away that you are tied fast into a fish, works more efficiently at Waitahanui than anywhere else I know. Like every other river or mouth in the world, this stream knows times when, despite the combined skill and patience of a hundred fishermen, the trout remain aloof. Gradually, over the next few days, the congregation of rods dwindles until, if you are lucky and persistent, it is possible to have one of the lower pools entirely to yourself. This state of affairs might well continue until eleven seconds from the time that you receive your first glorious strike. Like the raising of a floodgate the dam of fishermen descends upon the river and before your fish is landed or lost you will have newcomers' flies flailing your pool to a froth.

(There could be some truth in the story of the hairdresser who, by means of this eerie telepathy or because of particularly finely-tuned extrasensory perception, suddenly pocketed his scissors, locked the door from the outside and returned in triumph from Waitahanui

"The fish are running!" Shoulder to shoulder, cheek by jowl at the Waitahanui "picket fence".

three hours later to be berated by his only half-cut customer. It is harder however to give credence to the tale of the jeweller who, having received the same eerie message, thrust a tray of valuable diamond rings at a tantalisingly slow purchaser saying, "Here, take any one you want for five dollars, but please *hurry*.")

One man's meat is another's poison, and this is the way of the lower Waitahanui. Love it or loathe it. Enjoy fishing in a flock; or select another stream where you have the opportunity to find solitude. Choose the noise of passing cars, shrilling children, barking dogs and the top pop song on a blaring transistor; or find a stretch of water elsewhere where the elusive bellbird or tui provides the only background to the murmur of the stream. Accept a bit of early morning jostling for the last reasonable stance in deLatour's Pool immediately upstream from the bridge; or make the walk to the Cliff pool on the Tongariro where, at that time of the day, a couple of unwary rabbits are likely to be your only company. (A passing thought—does every river have a Cliff pool? The Tongariro does, the Waiotaka does, the Tauranga-Taupo, the Waitahanui—lack of imagination somewhere?) Prepare to spend your day with a fellow within a yard of either elbow and the thought in your mind that your ears protrude from your head to an alarming extent; or fish a secluded pool with a nymph on the upper reaches of the Waimarino. (The orange-bodied one on a number 12 hook, not the statuesque, cuddly manic variety.)

All of which will have given you the impression that the lower Waitahanui is not my favourite fishing spot. True. But, crafty fellow that I am, I have saved, like a child with the icing on the cake, the best until last.

The upper reaches of this charming river are a joy. Towering pumice cliffs bedecked with manuka and kanuka overlook the twisting, tortuous route which these deservedly famous waters take in their path to the lake, and the familiar pattern of pool, shallow, reach and run beckons anglers from throughout the world.

Waitahanui waters are the clearest of the extensive Taupo Basin, and when all other rivers and streams are unfishable because of heavy rainfall in the headwaters, this one remains untroubled and flood-free.

For those anglers who are prepared to walk upstream away from the madding throng which chokes the pools adjacent to the bridge, it is still possible to be rewarded with stretches of delightful river comparatively free of competition. Find them and one is more easily

Sundown at the Waitahanui rip. Newcomers join the "fence".

able to comprehend why so many will acknowledge no other waters than these. The occasional selfishness which insinuates itself in the downstream pools is seldom encountered among the upper river men. Perhaps it is because they have sought peace and solitude that they appear more gentle, more willing to assist the stranger, more prepared to sit and smoke and watch the stream chuckling by.

"Carrots" Kennedy, wife of Turangi's Dr Ron, tells a wry tale of the lack of camaraderie she experienced in deLatour's Pool a few years ago. The Tongariro and Waiotaka had been her choice for years and her skill with rod had made them successful years indeed. A change was indicated and the Waitahanui was selected. Long before dawn she was waiting at the poolside in the company of a couple of unseen and unknown competitors. The magic hour of five o'clock arrived and all made an exploratory cast into the darkness. Within seconds the spine-tingling whack of a strike whipped her rod downward and minutes later she had beached a gleaming fish in prime condition. There was no comment from her fellow anglers. Within minutes she was placing her second fish alongside the first. Again there was no reaction from the other two. It was to be one of those days. Another cast, another strike and again a fight successfully won.

This last fish proved too much for one of the still unrecognisable strangers. "Why the hell doesn't she stick to her own bloody river and leave Waitahanui to the regulars?" whined a voice from the gloom.

Not to this day does Carrots know who the regulars were but she felt she had aided the cause of Women's Lib to a pair of the opposite sex. Ms Greer would have been proud of her.

The aptly named Picket Fence at the mouth of the Waitahanui is not everyone's cup of tea but it is an experience to try at least once during an angling lifetime. How many tons of trout are beached from this outlet each year I have no means of knowing, but it must be enormous. With a run of fish gathering at the rip prior to spawning, you will have to be up betimes however to ensure an advantageous position.

I have done the Waitahanui far less than justice in devoting so few words to it, but since the 1940s and early 1950s I have fished it less than a dozen times. For those who crave more knowledge of it I "dips me lid" and refer them to Budge Hintz' *Trout at Taupo*. From him they will gain a much more intimate insight to the world-renowned pools of this lovely river.

The Stream Mouths

The eastern shoreline of Lake Taupo has fewer streams entering the watershed than the southern and western areas, and we have discussed the principal ones in this chapter. As with the Delta of the Tongariro, so do the rips of these rivers provide excellent year-round fishing given certain conditions. Many of you will have heard the old jingle which goes something like

When the wind's in the north, do not sally forth.
When the wind's in the west, the fish bite the best.
When the wind's in the east, the fish bite the least.
When the wind's in the south, it blows a fly down a mouth.

Having dredged that pearl up from the deep recesses of my mind, I have one recommendation to make: forget it. It's nonsense so far as Taupo is concerned. Probably it applied to Izaak Walton's England where the fishing camps he visited regularly faced due east and due north and the prevailing winds were from that quarter.

We get few easterlies in this area and if we do we are often experiencing rather more than indifferent weather. (Strangely, as I write this, I note the wind, such as it is, is from the east, and the day is glorious.) However, make a mental note of the easterly, for it will be your friendliest when fishing the mouths of the Waiotaka, Waimarino, Tauranga-Taupo and Hinemaiaia. I have stated before . . . or if I haven't I'll do so now . . . that especially with river mouth fishing I like the wind at my back, and not just because it makes casting easier.

The Waiotaka mouth is fairly shallow with no distinct lip, but uninspiring as it looks, let us not forget that the Waiotaka is a prodigious spawning stream and the trout must gather here before migration.

Begin casting whilst still on dry land, for often a fish or two, if undisturbed, will be lying in quite close. Lengthening your cast as you go, you can then proceed to move out down the current, fishing left and right, allowing the natural swing to work for you as you go. It is possible to wade for up to 50 yards from shore before the water level threatens the tops of your body waders. For the record, I find that during the hours of daylight the fish are generally well off shore, but during darkness they will often be lying in quite close. Probably night fishing is more productive, and I know many anglers who will not wet a line here except after dark. Regardless, I have enjoyed some wonderful sport throughout the day, and with access now made easy from the new Sailing Club entrance, combined with a low lake level, the long, and at times, swampy track which once was the only means of gaining the mouth, is eliminated.

Remember the wind. Easterly for preference, south-easterly for second choice, and a gentle southerly can also yield. Northerlies I have struggled with to little or no avail and westerlies will throw 4-foot waves at you guaranteed to either knock you over or fill your waders with Taupo's none-too-tropical waters. So much for the old wives' tale of *When the wind's in the west . . .*!

Upon going over these last few paragraphs again, I have made the discovery that practically all which has been said of the Waiotaka mouth applies equally to the Waimarino. The latter is a changeable creature inasmuch as there will sometimes be only one rip, at others two or even three. It matters not at all what you find upon arrival. Fish the inlet carrying the most water as first choice and experiment at leisure with the others. The shelf on to which the Waimarino flows is particularly shallow and it is possible, especially when the lake level is as low as it has been this year, to wade more than 100 yards down the rip. It's a long haul to land your fish but often they are lying over

Floatplane captain delivers clients and guide provides smoked trout lunch at Mission Bay.

the lip of the shelf in the deeper water and, if this is the case, a collapsible landing net is not a bad idea. You can then string them on your belt or on a cord around your waist.

The Tauranga-Taupo mouth presents a totally different proposition altogether, for here, like the Delta of the Tongariro, fishing from an anchored boat is permitted. It is probably a good thing too, for the lip is a steep and dangerous one which claimed two wading fishermen only three or four years ago.

Wind conditions which suit the Waiotaka and Waimarino are again favoured here, but the Tauranga-Taupo yields many more fish than the other two combined, in part because of its greater flow and the advantages of boat fishing. There are drawbacks however: generally, two boats in the heart of the rip will take 90 per cent of the fish caught in any one day and the others can do nothing but look on in envy and frustration. Unlike the Tongariro, this river has only one outlet and when the fish are gathering you have to be up almost before you've gone to bed to ensure a prime position. Even then, if you arrive at 4 am prepared to wait for the 5 o'clock legal start, there is no guarantee that you will not be the fourth or fifth boat in line. The bush telegraph seems to work better at the Tauranga-Taupo than anywhere else on the lake except the Waitahanui. It is possible at both inlets to have the water to yourself until you catch a fish. Then look out! The hordes descend as if they have merely been waiting in the bushes and under the pumice stones for the action to begin, and the Tauranga-Taupo mouth becomes a jostling mess of boats, gunwale to gunwale, similar to the shoulder-to-shoulder casting at the picket fence of the Waitahanui.

It's bad luck if you're wading when the boats make their appearance. Unless you strike a gentleman of the old school who allows you unimpeded passage for a cast, you are likely to be blocked off completely. It's hard to remonstrate too, for the boats are anchored just over the lip in the deep water and no trout is worth drowning for.

The inlet of the Hinemaiaia creates a good, strong, consistent rip, pleasant to wade, and it's one of my favourites. It isn't as crowded as the Waitahanui and although the anglers who work it regularly are competent and keen, there seems to be more friendliness among the competitors than a visitor to the Waitahanui rip might find.

Winds from between north-east and south-east are probably the best, but I have seen fish gather here on everything except a howling westerly or north-westerly.

Don't be too alarmed if you see a dozen or more cars parked under the trees in the summer, for Hatepe boasts a delightful beach which provides safe bathing for Mother and the kids, while Dad attempts to produce the evening meal of trout.

Yes, I know I have stated that my pride and joy is the Tongariro, but I also love a change. The smaller streams and their mouths will not only give you this, they will provide you with delightful fishing when the mood is upon them.

CHAPTER 12

TROLLING AND HARLING

To be blunt, I should state at the beginning of a chapter which deals with trolling that it is to me the least pleasurable method of catching trout. I have a friend who is so prejudiced against it that he describes it, with unconscious humour, as "going around and around in ever-diminishing circles until the inevitable occurs".

Trollers, I feel, can be placed in two categories. There are those who enjoy their summer holidays in the Taupo area, who possess a boat or a dinghy and often have a couple of young children whose delight at the prospect of water and boats and fishing is a joy to behold. They go trolling. Good luck to them, say I. During their two weeks' annual vacation, they will, if they are lucky or knowledgable, catch a few fish for the pan and have a couple left over to smoke and proudly present to friends when they return home. They have enjoyed memorable days on the lake, they have picnicked on sandy secluded beaches and they have given the kids the title of their first new-term essay—"How I Caught My First Rainbow Trout". They have achieved what they set out to do when they left the cares and the bustle of the city behind them. They have had fun.

And then there are the others, and these are a different breed altogether. They set out with one object in mind: to kill as many fish as possible in the shortest time possible. Many of them live within easy access of the lake, and on practically every day when Taupo is not reminiscent of the North Sea in a Force 8 gale, they are out in numbers. Trout of under 14 inches must be returned to the water throughout this district.

Do they admire one of 14½ inches and return it to the water with the thought in mind that it will be a better fish next year? They do not.

Do they keep as many fish as they can comfortably use, returning the others to live another day? As Eliza Doolittle remarked when she thought she was to be deprived of her taxi ride, "Not bloody likely!"

What on earth they do with all the trout they catch is beyond comprehension. Fertilise the garden? Make regular contributions to the overheads of boarding catteries? Inflict them *ad nauseam* upon the neighbours?

I don't know the answers to that one, but I know through experience that for a couple of months of the year, when fish are smelting freely, it is possible, sometimes without too much perseverance, to take a limit of trout on every rod in the boat day after day. Simple arithmetic will produce a total of 210 fish in one week by three trolling rods in one boat. That it does occur can not be disputed. That it must, in time, have a detrimental effect upon our freshwater fishing must, surely, be obvious.

Trollers of this latter group defend their actions by maintaining that the removal of a so-called "surplus" of fish from the lake maintains a balance by providing less competition for available food. With a sharply increasing number of anglers taking out licences each year, it might not be as long as we think before we face the situation in which so many other once-great trout countries now find themselves. Let us not forget that California originally supplied us with our first trout, and even Californians do not boast nowadays of their trout fishing. Of course, their population fostered industry, and with industry came the pollution of waterways, but disregard for the fish population also took its toll.

That pollution by enrichment is already evident in Lake Taupo there can be no doubt. Shallower areas, like Two Mile Bay in Taupo township itself, are progressively revealing more weed. It does not necessarily require an enormous population to nurture pollution. Even in a small town, the non-existence of a sewerage system, especially when the majority of the residential area is on hill slopes overlooking the lake, will provide the conditions upon which pollution will thrive.

Lake Rotorua and its problems have been discussed by far more able voices than mine. Already swimming is discouraged, it is recommended that trout be eaten only in small quantity, and a flight over the lake reveals a body of water which is far from the sparkling, clear basin it was only a few short years ago. Is the wonderful fishery of Taupo to suffer a similar fate? "Unlikely," many say, "it's too deep." It matters not if it were ten thousand feet deep in many places: one still wishes to utilise the shallow bays and inlets and find them free from contamination.

Reckless disregard for the numbers of fish killed will, in time,

The loneliness of the long-distance troller.

compound the affliction. Rarely during the best of the trolling season are adult fish caught. A significant majority are maiden fish, the following year's spawners. The argument culminates in a rhetorical question: exterminate the prospective parents, and where do you get your ova?

These maidens (often, I think mistakenly referred to as steelheads for a steelhead is named for his sea-going propensity) are the future lifeline of the whole freshwater fishery. Eradicate them in their thousands and we shall all repent at leisure. Take one or two for a breakfast dish, by all means, but if you wish your children and their children to enjoy the heritage you have learned to accept, spare the young fish at the expense of the older.

My kindest but severest critic, Jo—come to think of it, she is the only one to have read this far and that only because she types—has reminded me that I am on a hobbyhorse and riding it hard. "Wasn't," she enquired, "the heading of this chapter 'Trolling and Harling'? For the digression, I apologise. For the thoughts contained therein, I do not.

Because I am a guide there are times of the year, especially during midsummer, when I take the boat out on the lake and go trolling. Often the tourists I have on board have never fished for trout in their lives before, but with a day at their disposal and finding themselves in the midst of one of the world's finest trout areas, they are determined to try their luck. With so little time available, a day-long lesson in casting from the Delta or any other river mouth would prove frustrating and most likely, unrewarding. So, we go trolling.

I have already intimated that I prefer other methods of catching trout, but the delight on the faces of these visitors when finally a fish is netted, makes it all worth while. Almost without exception a startled gasp coincides with the sound of the reel's ratchet and a breathless request for further instruction. Inevitably, everything goes wrong. Both rod and reel handle are clasped in a grasp of such strength that one thinks immediately that the client is suffering a sudden paralysis. A hundred yards astern the boat a trout is leaping in an often successful attempt to free itself of what it had thought to be easy prey. Instructions on procedure, always at cross-purposes, are shouted from all sides. Sometimes, despite the commotion, the fish is landed.

For the identical reasons that I select, if possible, the windward shore when fly fishing I do the same when trolling. Not only is it more pleasant for both passengers and boatie when protected from wind and waves, but greater numbers of fish are caught. Additionally, the food supply is more often centred on this shore and I suggest, with not the slightest vestige of proof, that the trout's vision improves in calm sheltered water. Elsewhere, sand and debris are continuously clouding the water to the detriment of good feeding. Anyway, the theory seems to work fairly satisfactorily and I'll stick with it until someone comes along with a viable alternative.

One other factor which enables some fishermen to return day after day with tales and proof of success, when others are complaining bitterly that the fishing is not a patch on their previous visit in 1935, is that the former are prepared to study. I use the term "study" with consideration. There are a couple of extremely informative maps of Lake Taupo which reveal the depth of the lake at practically any given point. Without going to the trouble of purchasing one through the Marine Department, which is, incidentally, more informative, the Lands and Survey Department's "NZMS 116, Lake Taupo" is available from many booksellers and newsagents, especially in this area, and is worth about ten times its cost of 70 cents to the serious fisherman.

Unless smelting, fish feed predominantly on or near the bottom. If, therefore, you are trolling at a known depth, it is possible to approximate that level by the judicious use of a given amount of lead core or monel wire line. Of course, 100 yards of lead line will not go down to

Dad and lad prepare for trolling at Motutere Bay while mother and children are content to relax under a kowhai tree.

a depth within cooee of its length, but by working along the edge of a shelf with a depth which is already established, you will stand more chance of picking up a fish or two.

One other point: I'm a staunch advocate, especially with in-shore fishing, of the use of polarised glasses. Very often when there is glare on the water it is impossible for the naked eye to see the line of demarcation between shallow and deep. Before you know it, you are trolling over a shelf perhaps only 30 feet in depth with 100 yards of line behind the boat. The result is either a tedious reversal in an often vain result to free the lure or, as happens so often, a twanging sound as the line parts. Either way, the outcome is time-consuming and annoying.

Everyone I know who has had some measure of success when trolling is asked what particular spoon or spinner he has favoured that day. Probably because the troller is less likely to be an expert than the fly fisherman, the proficiency or the good fortune of the successful one is taken as a sign that he has a secret. Certainly a smaller percentage of fishermen catch the greater percentage of fish, but not always is it the choice of lure which determines this. More often, they know the lake well because they have done their homework. Purchase that map and study it.

Spinners, spoons and wobblers, like flies, come in a multitude of patterns, colours, shapes and sizes. On some days, all will take fish; on others, one type of one size only will attract. Frequently, especially when the trout seem determined to be uncooperative, I experiment, but usually finish up by at least commencing the day with the following types:

September-December inclusive: Flat fish (pale green and yellow), Black Toby, Mother of Pearl.
January-March inclusive: Black Toby, Green Toby, Cobra (green and gold, or brown and gold).

I really do apologise for the lack of reference to the remaining five months, but I don't recall having trolled during that period for many a year. The rivers are full of trout, the Delta is fishing well, and it's just too cold and often wet, to be sitting around in a boat without activity.

There are times when a trolled fly will produce when spinners are being ignored. During the smelting season when fish are active on the surface and close inshore or on the shallow shelves, a fly line trolled about 30 yards behind the boat can be deadly. Practically any fly which resembles a smelt in size will be effective, but of them all I prefer those tied on a no. 8 or no. 10 hook: Parson's Glory, Bishop's Blessing, Green Smelt, Silver Rabbit, and Grey Ghost.

All, I feel, should be sparsely dressed with a minimum of hackle to permit the body colour to be easily distinguished. The Parson's Glory and the Green Smelt seem to work better if tied with silver tinsel wrapped around the respective body colours—the others are silver-bodied anyway.

Harling is a term which is, I think, peculiar to this country. Certainly Americans elevate their eyebrows when the word is used. Quite simply, of course, it is a form of trolling using ordinary fly fishing tackle from a moving boat. Strip off between 25 and 50 yards of line, find an area where fish are feeding on or close to the surface, and move in amongst them. During the hot summer months this method can be extremely effective, especially in early mornings and evenings.

There will be times of course when the smelting fish are working further out and you wonder whether your fly line is reaching far enough under the surface to make contact. It is possible on such occasions to experiment with your trolling gear, paying out, say,

30 yards of line to start with. The same flies on your rig as you had used on the fly rods will often begin to yield fish when, only a few minutes, before they were being treated with disdain.

Whether trolling or harling I'm an advocate of a particularly long leader. By this, I mean something in the nature of 30 feet or more. I'm sure that the lure is delivered of more movement with this length of monofilament and, of course, it is further removed from the heavy and obvious line. At the other end of the scale I once came across a fellow having the devil of a time trying to fit a 40-lb test lead-core line directly into the eye of a fly. I looked around, saw the new boat waiting at the launching ramp, the new rod and reel and, by her age and shyness, a new wife as well. Nobody had told him the facts of life so far as fishing was concerned. For his attractive wife's sake I hope he knew the others.

When compared with trolling, which generally utilises lead-core lines, harling has many attractions. Firstly, the fish, once hooked, is fought on a fly rod, which is about a thousand times more fun than on some of the trolling rods used. These more often than not would make excellent broom handles. Secondly, the trout strikes close to the surface and is almost always acrobatic and visible. Again, it enables a fisherman who is an inept caster to have the feel of a fish on light equipment, and it eliminates that heavy and arduous cranking of the reel to retrieve 100 or more yards of lead line.

I much prefer the joy of casting to trout, but if asked to fish from a moving boat, harling has it all over trolling in so far as enjoyment is concerned.

One encounters many humorous moments when guiding, and probably they occur more frequently when trolling than at any other time. Which is not too surprising, when about a quarter of the clients have never previously fished for trout.

An elderly and delightful lady from New Mexico employed me for three days a couple of seasons ago. She had fished throughout the world, not only for trout, but also for marlin, bonefish, tuna, yellow-tail and every other marine speedster you could think of. Accompanying her was her companion-help, secretary, general factotum, and dogsbody, all rolled into one package in the form of a pleasant but rather naive spinster of uncertain age.

My client expressed a preference for fishing from a boat and we set sail for Stump Bay, where I had seen fish smelting only the previous day. Within half an hour we had found fish in quantity and the elderly expert, hooked, played skilfully and landed three whilst harling. Meantime, I had been instructing the companion in the intricacies of playing a fish when one should strike, and ended with my usual warning: "If the fish runs, take your hand off the reel and let it run. Hold on to the reel handle and you'll break it off for sure."

She nodded her understanding and once again I took the boat around to the working fish. Surely enough it was the hired help's turn for a strike. She followed my instruction to the letter. Her right hand was not endeavouring to clutch the madly spinning reel. With an "O my God" she also removed her left hand from the rod handle at the same time, tossing my Feralite in the air. My client and I made a grab simultaneously but it was too late. Rod, reel, line and fish all disappeared into 60 feet of blue lake. There was a long silence. We peered overboard as if by some miracle the process could be reversed as a film can be run backwards. My client looked stonily at her companion: "You silly witch," she said, and my quotation misses the actual by only one letter. There followed a harangue which occupied a full five minutes, all in particularly unladylike language and which contained many references to the secretary's shortcomings in all walks of life.

Considering my client had appeared both charming and a little prim before this episode I was more than a trifle shocked. America, I realised, had what they call cuss-words totally foreign to a New Zealander. She did, however, leave no doubt as to their meaning. The eventual silence was long and embarrassing. I made what I hoped were suitable clucking noises and endeavoured to give the impression that this sort of thing happened every day. That evening, when the atmosphere had warmed a little over a couple of large martinis, the secretary excused herself for a moment. My client asked the cost of replacement of the equipment: I suggested 50 dollars and she produced a traveller's cheque for 100.

"The other fifty," she said, "is for letting me have the first good swear I've indulged in for many a year. You know, when you reach seventy-seven, people expect you to act like the First Lady at a banquet to raise funds for the next presidential election. I make a point of not letting her know that I find her completely indispensable. She's capable, honest, hardworking and Godfearing," she added, and then with a wink as wicked as it was comical, she asked, "And did you ever see anyone blush to that colour before?"

Trolling *de-luxe*. Young couple troll close (too close for the regulations ?) to the backdrop of the Waihi Falls.

I raised my glass to her. "I'll bet she outfishes you in the next two days."

"You're on," she said.

Try as we might, we did not succeed in making even a moderately successful angler out of the companion and, as I had guessed, I lost my wager.

Trout are where you find them when trolling, for they are fairly evenly scattered throughout the lake, but if they can be taken in shallower water without the necessity of using 100 yards or more of line, the fishing will be more pleasurable. Let's face it: even with the assistance of a 5-inch reel, it takes a considerable amount of physical exertion to retrieve a length of line equal to an Olympic dash, especially when the fish is not on your line but your neighbour's. There are times, however, mainly during extremely hot weather when the trout are down deep, and then one must chase them and be darned to the effort.

There are days out there on the tranquil water beneath the high cliffs of the western boundary of our beautiful Taupo, when merely to reflect upon one's great good fortune in having so lovely a lake at the back door, is joy indeed. We take our lake and the rivers which feed it so much for granted as our natural inheritance that it surprises us when visitors from overseas react in delighted amazement at the clarity of our water. Many of them have discovered, to their horror, that a visit to a lake or stream they enjoyed and loved in their youth is a shattering experience. Childhood memories, tinged with nostalgia and perhaps even a little exaggeration, are precious as we become older, and to have them rudely sundered leaves a scar which will remain forever. Too late they have discovered the meaning of the words pollution, enrichment, litter, weed and odour when applied to natural waters. All too often they are confronted with signs which state "It is inadvisable . . ."; "No Swimming"; "Fish from this area should not be eaten or taken away"; "Do not drink".

More often than I can recall I have been asked if the water from Lake Taupo is fit for drinking and, upon replying in the affirmative, have had one of my clients remark "But isn't that just too wonderful, Hortense? Fancy not even having to boil it first!"

Boil Taupo water? God forbid I shall ever see the day. . . .

CHAPTER 13

THE SMELTING SEASON

It is a week short of Christmas Day and after a busy November, the garden is even more neglected than it habitually is. Following a month's idleness the lawnmower has been obstinate to an infuriating degree in its reluctance to start. The air is blue when it finally coughs into life. Two strips later and Jo tells me I am wanted on the telephone. Mumbling, I slip it into neutral and say a short prayer that it will not stall.

"Hello?" I growl.

"Hi, Tony," says Bill, or Tom, or Jack, or any one of a couple of dozen fishing friends. "Just thought I'd let you know the fish are smelting at the Sandspit."

It is perhaps an hour afterwards when I begin to wonder whether I had the courtesy to thank him for the information, or did I just cradle the receiver without a word? More likely the latter, I decide as I cast a Silver Rabbit no. 10 ahead of half a dozen swirling trout only 20 feet from shore. Never mind, I'll ring him later in the evening with an apology and he will understand, for he is a fisherman and knows the strange madness which overcomes all anglers at the mention of smelting fish.

Earlier we discussed the introduction of smelt into Lake Taupo as an additional source of food supply for the trout, Every year around the stream mouths and in sheltered bays millions of the tiny fish hatch and the trout indulge in a feeding frenzy similar to that of schools of sea fish when attacking bait. For those of you who have yet to experience it, it is difficult to describe the excitement of standing, often only ankle-deep in water, watching a black shadow of perhaps 200 trout herd the little fish into a dense mass and then smash into them mercilessly. To make your cast, to move the clearly visible lure and see a trout peel off from the school, accelerate with astonishing speed and make the strike is an experience no angler should be allowed to miss. To make your cast, to have the same

The trout are smelting. Father works Motutere Bay while the family await results.

sequence of events follow and to have him turn away at the last possible moment is almost as exciting. On some days they are nearly suicidal in their determination to take anything which moves, natural or artificial; on others they can be infuriatingly selective. On Monday they will not hesitate to accept any one of a dozen different lures; on Tuesday you will tie on everything in your box at least twice for only a meagre return. On Wednesday a limit of 10 fine, fat fighting fish; on Thursday a couple of worn-out long, lean kelts that a cat would refuse with disdain. But, and it's a big but, the days which are good are glorious and during the 10 or 12 weeks of smelting activity there are many of them.

The start of this particular phenomenon varies a little from season to season, presumably with lake conditions affecting the timing of the smelt hatch. In 1971, the action began around the third week of October, which is early by normal standards and that was an exceptional year—in 1972 it was not evident until the beginning of December and was poorer than any other I can recall. Of 1973, I am dubious. I hope my prophecy is wrong, but I forecast another indifferent season based on the falling lake level, which this year is the lowest in recorded history. Should it continue to decline throughout the smelt spawning, much of the ova will be left high and dry to perish. Let us hope for good winter rains.

Mediocre or outstanding, however, the blood still tingles at the message, "The fish are smelting".

Choice of line is probably more important than the selection of the appropriate fly for this type of fishing. Again, I lean toward the sinking tip, but a floater or a slow sinker will do the job well. Don't then, go out and buy a sinking tip merely for the smelting season, although as mentioned previously, it's a grand line if you are enthusiastic about nymphing. One word of warning when buying one, however: try, if you can, to get one which will be easily seen when lying on the water. Green is too difficult to pick up on a dull day, but I recently acquired a line of this type which the manufacturers call "hot orange". It's a dandy, and is clearly visible on overcast days or even in cloudy water.

November, December, January. Writing this as I am in the heart of winter, those summer days seem far away, and yet, when they do arrive we shall be doubly blessed. To be able to pursue one of the truly delightful fishing experiences any angler could dream about, and to follow the sport in a short-sleeved shirt and barefooted if so desired, is my idea of bliss.

The novice, having whetted his appetite by listening to enthusiasts discussing the smelting season is, naturally enough, going to say "Fine, but where the devil do I find these Kamikaze fish?" Perhaps the simple answer is to apply the old axiom of keeping the wind at your back. Smelt will select a sheltered shoreline wherever they can, and where the smelt are the trout will follow. At our (southern) end of Lake Taupo, undoubtedly the winds to bring the fish in close are the westerlies and south-westerlies. Unpleasant as it may be for casting, the harder it blows the better and the more likely you are to be rewarded. If you do not have a boat, there are still many spots where your car will carry you to within easy access of good fishing. Heading west from Turangi, Slip Creek, which is reached from the Waihi road just beyond Tokaanu, Waihi Falls, Omori Stream and Kuratau Stream all fish well, with the latter most favoured. It's a strange spot, this Kuratau rip. It is well sheltered from all except strong northerlies and easterlies, and trout are nearly always in evidence. Too much so at some times, for I have seen the water literally boiling with feeding fish and a dozen rods excitedly hammering away at them, but to no avail. On other days, lads of tender years will borrow Dad's rod for an hour and come home dragging two or three handsome fish through the dust. Some days those Kuratau trout are as educated as Einsteins, on others they must be the dumbest fish in the lake.

I took a client out there one blustery December day a couple of years ago. One look and he was prepared to seek other pastures, for there were fully two dozen rods working the mouth and the rip. Ladies in summer frocks and enormous straw sun-hats were making vigorous if unscientific efforts to project a line without endangering themselves or their near neighbours. Small boys with bare legs and short pants wet to the waist were using trolling rods with half-inch tips to float a fly down the current or flog the water to foam. Further out, a dozen men were working the rip with practised precision and total dedication.

"This I can do without," said my man. "This I can get any Sunday back in California." We were standing in the car park about 40 yards from the water as he spoke and I grinned when I said, "Let's take a closer look as long as we're here." We sauntered down to the lake edge. His jaw dropped and his eyes started to bug.

"Are those fish I see jumping?" he exclaimed.

"Those are fish," I told him. "Hundreds of fish. I guessed that if the frail and the infirm, the babies and the grandmothers were fishing, there must have been a bunch of trout in here smelting."

A bunch, did I say? There were hundreds upon hundreds of fish, rolling, swirling, smashing, clearing the water in all their silvery magnificence, some only inches from shore, some a full quarter-mile distant.

At that moment two men in the rip commenced the walk back to the bank, rods bowed in that graceful arc which denotes success, and within 10 feet of us a rather more capable lady angler than the others struck a fish which leapt once and, leaving her lamenting, departed with her fly.

"Well, we'd better move on and find a less congested spot," I suggested as a couple of fish swirled only 20 feet out.

"Move on?" he roared at me. "What the hell do you mean, move on?"

"But you said something about Californian Sundays and that you—" but it was no use. I was talking to myself. Ken Woods, for that was his name—and he will have recognised himself if he ever reads this chapter—was already off at an undignified gallop towards the car. I went to help him mount his rod and select a fly. It was as well I did: he was tense, nervous, and what with shaking hands and glances over his shoulder towards the lake, it is doubtful if he would have been fishing within the hour.

"Move on?" he kept mumbling, "Move on, when I've never seen as many fish in my life? There are more trout down there than I knew the world contained. O God! *Move on*!"

He tottered down to the lake in a daze, incredulous. Fish wallowed left and right. He made his cast, a short one, the fly hit the water, a trout hit the fly and Ken's greatest afternoon of trout fishing had begun. He could do no wrong. Wherever he flung that green-bodied smelt imitation there was action. He moved along the beach from the crowd and like the rats following Hamelin's Pied Piper the fish followed him. He was not a prodigious caster. He didn't need to be. He didn't even wet his feet. He didn't have to. (And here, my friends is something we shall pursue further in a moment.) Big fish, smaller fish, fat fish and lean fish, Ken played the tune and they all came running.

He retired from the fray at 7 o'clock. He simply sat down on the now cooling sand, groped for a cigarette, lit it, and looking up at me through the blue haze said, "I don't believe it. I simply don't believe it. They told me you guys had the best trout fishing left in the world, but this is not of this world. I've died, and I'm in a special compartment of Heaven reserved for fishermen. If I never catch another trout in my life, I shan't ever mind."

It sounded sentimental, but it was said with such simplicity, such sincerity, that one forgot that many of his countrymen are sentimentalists when faced with the simple, the unspoiled, the beautiful.

"I've caught over twenty fish in four hours, more or less," he continued. "Not little, pale, feeble, hand-raised, follow-the-liberation-truck fish, but trout. T-R-O-U-T. Beautiful, big fighting trout."

For my part, it was easy to see he was still in a state of shock, but it was better to leave him that way. The morrow would possibly prove to him that smelting fish do not often oblige like that.

And the 20 fish he caught when the limit is 10? Nineteen he turned loose as soon as he landed them. One he kept for the chef at the Turangi Hotel to work her wonders upon.

"How was it?" I enquired the next day.

"Ambrosia," he said, and his eyes glazed once more.

In the event, Ken was one of two anglers I have had from overseas

Casting for smelting fish from a drifting boat at Bulli Point.

who has taken a limit of fish over three days or more on Lake Taupo with a fly rod. The other was my good friend and fine angler Lester Colby whom you have met before. Is Ken returning? You can offer a shade of odds on that one, and my only wish is that he doesn't expect exactly the same cooperation on his next visit.

So much for the Kuratau. You will either have a ball or have them bouncing against your waders and sneering at your efforts.

Two days of a westerly blow, a summer evening and I start to picture what might be going on at Slip Creek, Waihi Falls or the Omori Stream mouth. All have shallow rocky bottoms where they join the lake, which might account for the fact that they fish far better at night than they do in the daylight hours, for if you can see trout, more often than not, they can see you. Which brings me back to Ken and his 20 fish and the fact that he didn't get his feet wet whilst taking them. He let the smelting fish come to him instead of charging out into the middle of them and pushing them further out with every step he took.

I think and hope that I am fairly slow to anger, but there's one type in particular whose life is in immediate danger from drowning. He is the character—no, the fool—no, the hopeless idiot—who, with fish rising freely in shallow water, barges in among them to the top of his waders. He is the one, who, five minutes later, complains that the trout are rising beyond casting distance. If you point out to him that he has been the cause of the situation, he replies to the effect that anyone who stands high and dry is not really fishing anyway. Not for this nitwit the thrill of actually seeing the fish suddenly turn and with powerful strokes of a strong tail speed, mouth agape in anticipation, at a well presented imitation. Out into the deep for him, fishing blind, herding trout in front of him like a well-trained sheep dog with a mob of timid hoggets.

Night fishing does not hold the interest for me which once it did, but a pleasant summer evening with a few fish rising at any of these mouths can be a wonderful experience. And if you stay until after dark there's always the chance that you will tangle with that giant brown, which, though not the scrapper pound-for-pound that the rainbow is, is something to have photographed or mounted or both. Posterity may never see the like.

Midway between Omori and Kuratau the Sandspit, shown on the map as Te Rae Point can, and often does produce some of the best smelt fishing on the lake. Astonishing, fabulous fishing.

Forming a right angle as it does, one side or the other is favoured according to the wind. Quite simply you fish the deep or easterly-facing bank in a westerly or north-westerly, and the northern shore-line when the prevailing sou'westerly or southerly is piping. It's gentlemanly fishing too, from a pleasant sandy beach with ample room for a backcast and invariably an interested band of spectators guaranteed to obstruct you either physically or verbally at the critical moment of beaching your fish. It was not *homo sapiens* however who lost Jo a fish this past season. She and I had taken a drive to see if anything was moving around the lake, and coming to the Sandspit we released our rods from the car clips and wandered around the beach, keeping an eye open for a rise. A couple of anglers were worrying the water off the point and informed us that they hadn't seen a fish broach in hours. As if to prove them evaders of absolute truth, a couple of fish rose within 20 yards or so of where we were standing.

"Let's have a crack at those," I suggested.

She was already peeling line off the reel and tossed out a fly in the general direction. Too short. The second cast had the distance and she started the fast retrieve essential to successful smelt fishing. A few pulls and bingo! It wasn't a large fish, but with its first leap it was obvious that it was thoroughly annoyed. Jo played it as well she knows how and gradually the fight swung her way. Into the shallow she drew him until his head was safely on the sand. Moving forward maintaining a high rod and good steady pressure she was within 10 feet of him when a bouncing, excitedly barking golden Labrador burst on to the scene. Oblivious to everything but the strange, flapping creature which might provide endless fun as a playmate, the crazy canine failed to see the leader. Thumping it at 40 miles per hour or thereabouts had the inevitable result. The hook tore from the skin of the trout's jaw like a skin from a banana: reprieved at the eleventh hour the fish gave one last convulsive flip, felt her own blessed environment once more and slowly took off for safer shores. Both Jo and the dog looked disappointed momentarily but, like the good sport she is, it was only seconds before the funny side of it struck her. We roared. The dog was a sport too. He brought me a stick to throw so that he could show his prowess as a retriever. We became firm friends from the moment I obliged.

The Pukawa Stream mouth occasionally plays host to fish working smelt, but it is one of those things that one often hears about and rarely experiences. To me it has always been one of those "you-should-have-been-here-on Friday" areas, although I do know that the night fishing can be quite extraordinary.

These, then, are the areas on the southern and western shores of the lake which are comfortably reached by car, but the whole of the eastern side provides splendid smelting providing the wind is in the right quarter. Around all the river mouths, Hallett's Bay, Mission Bay, Motutere, Stump Bay—at any or all of these areas you may find working fish. Just stop the car, grab your rod and proceed to enjoy yourself.

I suppose it is when western bays are discussed that one starts to drool at the prospect of a wonderful day's outing with tremendous sport in the offing. Probably because so many inlets are difficult of access except by boat, one imagines that on this particular day of all days, the choice of stream mouth will be free of competition. Rarely is it so. From Whareroa—which we shall include as we pass it on the way around to the Whanganui, further on to Waihaha and so on to Waihora we shall be more than fortunate if there are not already two or three boats drawn up on the beach at each inlet. During smelting, however, the trout are generally fairly mobile and are not always confined to the rip. Of a consequence, wandering along the beach can often be more productive than standing in the one spot all day.

Whareroa is a favourite of mine. It is one of those areas where the fish are noticeable only by their absence or the water is being churned to a froth. Not a tug on the line for a couple of hours of casting or action aplenty every few minutes. The Whareroa flows into a particularly shallow bay and here again it is a definite disadvantage to wade out deep and start your casting. Remain comparatively high and dry and the fish will come to you. Burst your way out to your armpits and you'll push them in front of you until they are out of range. And it takes a long while for them to return, too.

Stories of fabulous days at the Whareroa are legend and I've been lucky enough to experience a number myself. Days like those my friend Ken encountered at the Kurutau. Days when the trout seemed actually to prefer the artificial to the dinkum oil. On such occasions choice of fly doesn't seem of paramount importance and even although I am having success with one particular pattern, the fellow 20 yards along the beach is doing equally as well with something totally different.

Probably a selection of the following will be included in your box: Rabbit (silver body), Grey Ghost, Blondie, Parson's Glory, Taupo Tiger, Smelt (green body). I like them tied on hook sizes 10 or 12 and certainly nothing bigger than an 8. Of course, as with river flies, there will be hoards of fishermen who have their favourites which are not included in these patterns, but for a short list of half a dozen, these will suffice. One word of warning here, when casting the Parson's Glory, Grey Ghost or Smelt: in windy conditions check the tail or streamer of the fly every few casts. Being soft and pliable they are liable to wrap around the shank of the hook, and no self-respecting trout is going to look at a lure which gives the impression of being a contortionist.

Select, if you can, a westerly wind for the Whareroa, and if it has been blowing for two or three days before your visit, so much the better. The angler is fairly well protected from a nor'-westerly too by the curve of the bay, but I've had little success on anything other than these two winds.

Occasionally you will see an odd fish lying in the stream proper. Don't be tempted to toss a fly in its general direction, for the regulations state quite plainly that the Whareroa is prohibited water. You just never know when Big Brother in the form of a ranger could be watching.

A mere couple of miles or so beyond the Whareroa, having passed sheer and beautiful cliffs plunging down into the clearest water you are ever likely to see, is one of the most delightful coves of the Taupo

Otupotu Falls. A magnificent backdrop to a superb fishing area.

basin. Never has such an attractive spot deserved its name more —Scenic Bay. Semicircular in shape, it is protected from all but a steady northerly breeze, and although inclined to be overcrowded with picnickers and water skiers at weekends, high days and holidays, it still plays host to smelting fish in numbers when conditions are favourable. Native forest, green and lush, towers above the white sand beach, birdcalls come pleasantly to the ear. A place where it matters not a jot if the fish are rising, for the sand is warm and inviting, there is shade for the eyes, and no boudoir ever had such perfect surroundings for a midday siesta.

Venture beyond Scenic Bay, down past Karangahape Cliffs, immense and awe-inspiring, and you find some of Taupo's most unspoiled and grand vistas. Exciting, wonderful country. You will of course have been prudent, for now you are far from home and Taupo can be big and temperamental and dangerous when the mood takes her. You will have checked the weather forecast for the day and made certain that a relatively thin line of dark cloud does not smear the western hills, for this is often a portent of strong winds to follow.

On only a couple of occasions have I been caught in a small craft on Taupo when the weather has deteriorated rapidly, and it is not an experience I am in any great hurry to repeat. The waves appear suddenly, frighteningly, seemingly rushing in from a variety of quarters, funnelling through saddles in the surrounding cliffs. Often unpredictable, at one moment your bow is comfortably up into them, at the next white water is rushing down at you on either beam. It doesn't happen often, this sudden change, but when it does, you will remember it for a long time to come. Much of the equipment which the authorities advise is essential in small boats may at times seem so much extra impedimenta, but through bitter experience they know what is necessary. There is a small pocketbook readily available from booksellers entitled *Safety In Small Craft*, which advises what should be carried on your boat. Buy it for a few cents and adopt its recommendations. If you can't find it, the local harbour master will be only too happy to oblige.

Whanganui, Waihaha, Waihora: names made famous by the quality of the fishing they have provided over the years. If ever you are fortunate enough to find them free from competition, you could well imagine yourself in another world.

Now we are led to understand that the owners are to "develop" both Whareroa and Waihaha, subdividing the land into building sections, forming good access roads from main highways, creating further playgrounds in the wilderness. It is sad, desperately sad, but if the developers cannot give rise to a phoenix let us hope they will endeavour to retain as much of the natural splendour as is humanly possible. There is so little of our area which has not been despoiled by the advance of the bulldozer immediately adjacent to the lake edge that our grandchildren, if not our children, will never know the meaning of serenity and solitude when the terms are applied to Lake Taupo.

"Progress," some will say.

"Yuk," say I.

Fly fishing is not the only method of catching fish at this stage of the year. Certainly, to me, the most enjoyable, but more often than I wish to recall the fish have been on the move well out in the deep, dark blue water and, wait as one will, they show no tendency to oblige by moving closer to the shoreline. Nor, cantankerous creatures that they are, will they venture in any numbers close to your drifting or slowly moving boat. At such times harling a Parson's

Glory or Bishop's Blessing (which I find an outstanding harling fly when tied with the silver body, not the gold) some 40 yards astern is the next best thing to lethal. In passing, I should mention that I understand the above flies were named after a Mr Parson and a Mr Bishop respectively, in the same manner that Mr Pope was responsible for Pope's Nondescript. Perhaps one day a genuine member of the clergy will come up with a winner which can justly be titled Curate's Egg or Vicar's Quicker or Reverend's Reliable?

The method is far from a purist's idea of tangling with trout, but if your wife has given you permission to have a day on the lake on the understanding that she can invite in the neighbours for an evening's fish fry, it will almost guarantee a return trip next week. It will, so to speak, get you off the hook.

You might not have cast to the fish, you almost certainly will not have seen it take your fly, but at least having felt the strike you will be fighting it on equipment designed to give the trout some chance of a fair fight. And, needless to say, you will keep only those fish which you can comfortably use—or will you?

During the smelting season trolling can be and, more often than not is, mass murder. Choice of equipment is simple. A 3-foot, solid glass rod with a tip diameter of at least half an inch, a reel of not less than 5-inch diameter, 100 yards or more of monel wire or lead-core line, 20 feet of 30-lb breaking strain leader and a 3-inch piece of hardware on the end of the lot.

This type of tackle simplifies things considerably. In the first place, there is no chance of the fish breaking off, so we don't have to let it run. Providing our arms are sufficiently strong we can just winch them straight in. Secondly, the rod is indestructible so it doesn't matter if our clumsy feet tread on it a few times a day. Thirdly, if we really work at it, it should be possible to retrieve all the line in 2 minutes and 14 seconds flat providing the fish is under 13 pounds 5 ounces. Thus, allowing for the odd can of beer which will be tossed nonchalantly over the side upon completion, we should be able to take our limit in about 1 hour 10 minutes. Great stuff. Of course we shall never really know what trout fishing is all about, but they will be in the boat. We shall never know the thrill of playing a fish, but we shall have a new record for the time it took us to drown it. And we shall be able to say when we return, "These Taupo fish aren't so wonderful. That six-pounder there didn't even put a bend in the rod."

Enough nonsense. The point I am trying to make is simple: buy equipment which will enable you to feel your fish and thus enjoy your fishing. Use tackle which will at least give the trout a chance. Don't use a rod which would have enabled Captain Ahab to whip Moby Dick. Don't use leaders that would hoist a groper from the 200-fathom mark.

And lastly, if we are not to be faced with closed seasons and other restrictions on these wonderful waters of ours, it will be to our advantage to remember the motto of the Fly Fishermen's Federation: "Limit Your Kill; DON'T Kill Your Limit."

CHAPTER 14

LAKE ROTOAIRA

IT IS SELDOM I issue a challenge, but I am tempted to make it international when I think of Rotoaira. With my limited knowledge of fishing in say, Alaska or Chile or Argentina or Ecuador, I am reluctant to "put my dollars where my mouth is", but here goes. Show me a lake to outfish New Zealand's Rotoaira and I shall acknowledge the greatest provider of trout for a minimum of effort in the world. Take me up on it and of course I shall require air fares and a generous expense account to satisfy myself of your claim, but if you're confident this should be no barrier. Winner to receive a Jaguar for his mother-in-law. (How much are those big cats anyway?) Loser to wear a badge entitled "I don't know what I'm talking about" for twelve months.

The early morning or late evening summer fishing in this charming 6-square-mile body of water has to be experienced to be believed. Taciturn business magnates have become hysterical in my presence, the elderly implore that we go home before they suffer a coronary, the excitable merely faint. Cast upon successive cast will produce a strike. It is unbelievable, ridiculous, but so often true.

Rotoaira, steeped in Maori history, is one of the few bodies of water still owned and administered by the Maori people, and despite offers from Government to purchase it as an integral part of the Tongariro power scheme the local Tuwharetoa tribe, which manages it under a Trust, has stuck to its guns. Relationships between the owners and various government departments have not always been cordial, but most of the problems appear to have been eliminated to mutual satisfaction. As things stand at the moment, the Trust is making a good thing out of it, as any business tries to do, the Government is using the lake as a holding dam for its project, the fishing is as fabulous as ever, and everyone is calling everyone else a damned fine fellow, which is the way things should be but seldom are.

Situated 12 miles south of Turangi on Highway 47, the lake is a

Lake Rotoaira with Motuopuhi Island in the foreground and Mt Tongariro as a snowcapped backdrop.

temperamental hussy depending on the wind. Placid, serene, inviting in the early light, she can become cold, thoroughly unpleasant company by afternoon. Not a ripple to disturb the reflections at dawn, frozen spray and white-capped waves a couple of hours later. She will humour you for days on end, cast her spell and her bounty over you and then, as suddenly, deny you access. But catch her in her good moods and she will give you the angling experience of a lifetime.

They don't often run to giants, these Rotoaira fish; indeed I doubt that the average would better 3½ lb, but when they are on the take they are nothing short of voracious. It's not because they're skinny, underfed, puny trout either—these fellows are short, deep, well-nourished and, pound for pound, force a battle beyond their size. They take a fly as if it were the last one left in the lake, and because the fly fishermen habitually work among the shallow weed beds, the trout spend more time out of the water than in it. And fish like that are always exciting. Eight, ten or a dozen jumps 3 feet clear of the water are the rule rather than the exception. If you fish as light in tackle as I like to on these waters, you can wave your fish and fly goodbye if you do not remember to drop your rod tip when he explodes.

Captain Stu Apte of Miami, Florida, world-renowned guide of sportsmen chasing the big tarpon on the Keys is one of the only men

I know to regularly accomplish this as second nature. World record holder of these monsters on a fly rod, Stu has actually boated a 151 pounder, and built into the leader was a section of 12 lb breaking strain monofilament! As he puts it, "If you don't bow to the silver king," his pet name for the mighty, leaping tarpon, "you might as well pack up your broken tackle and go home." What he means, naturally, is that as the fish makes its leap, the rod tip must be lowered to take the tension out of the leader. Imagine a fish as large as that falling from 6 feet or more on to a taut 12-lb section of leader. To a lesser degree the same principle applies when a trout leaps, especially when you are fishing as light as Stu does. I don't remember him using a tippet strength of more than 2 lb in any of our local waters and he hooks, plays and lands more fish than any other three men. He has taught me a lot during his fairly regular visits with his delightful and beautiful Bernice, and I am much indebted to him. A wonderful angler with a tremendous reservoir of fishing lore, and a great guy to boot.

Rotoaira is generous to all types of fishermen. Fly-rodders, spin-casters and trollers all do well, so let's take them in order and try and describe methods and sites for those of you who haven't fished it previously.

With the prevailing winds between sou'west and nor'west most fly men launch the boat at the new ramp where custodian Bob Biddle has his home and office and proceed up beyond the island of Motuopuhi, once a strongly fortified Maori pa. It is difficult as one skirts its perimeter and enjoys the shade of its overhanging bush to

Lester Colby from Montana, USA, with his $10\frac{1}{4}$ pound rainbow from Lake Rotoaira.

imagine that this now peaceful and lovely isle was many times the centre of bloody and merciless warfare.

Once beyond the island a line of buoys indicates that shoreward is reserved for anchored boat fishing only. In other words you may cast from a stationary boat with either fly rod or spinning rod but you are not permitted to drift or troll. The rule is broken on occasion, but don't let Bob intercept you while doing it. He's a hard man to escape too, for his new jetboat travels like the wind.

Outcrops of weed rise above the surface of the lake and it is in the channels between these that I normally drop the anchor. The weed-banks are full of crustaceans—mainly snails—and the trout feed heavily among them. It is rarely deeper in these parts than 15 or 20 feet and a line which does not go down like a stone is recommended. Once again I use that same old sinking tip, for there is nothing more frustrating than having to remove weed from the hook and leader cast after cast. Incidentally, although I have no absolute proof to substantiate it, I go along with every other angler I know, when saying that no fish will attack a fly or spinner which is trailing weed, or anything else for that matter.

There is a nervousness and a shakiness of hands about the first few casts of the day, for often the glassy surface of the lake will be covered in dimples and rings and swirls and splashes, some almost alongside the boat, some as far away as the eye can see. Make your cast, let it settle a few moments and begin the retrieve, not too quickly at first, about one foot at a time. Vary it a little next time, and again the next, until you meet that glorious resistance which is unmistakably the strike of a fish. By the time you have seen him leave the water half a dozen times, coaxed him, heart in mouth, back through a dense weedbed, had him wrap himself once around the anchor warp, dive under the boat, and missed him twice as you attempt to net him, you will have completely forgotten what particular retrieve had enticed him anyway. Back through the pattern again.

When Rotoaira fish are really on the feed they appear to take just about any old fly in the box. I've seen four anglers, side by side, all too busy to talk, each using a different lure. Those fish, when in the mood, attack anything that moves into their vision, whether it is big, small or medium, orange, green or puce. Time without number, I have had a client take time out to light a cigarette or gulp a cup of coffee rapidly cooling off, and a trout has accepted his lure which has been sitting innocuously on the water not 5 feet from the boat. The

Rex Forrester works the Whakapapanui Stream as Mt Ngauruhoe prepares for a major eruption in the background.

"Thar she blows!" Mt Ngauruhoe belches ash in the direction of Lake Rotoaira. Minutes later the guide's boat was covered in the ash.

result is, of course, hilarious. Burnt fingers or a showerbath of coffee.

Probably the flies most generally used are Turkey and Green, Red Setter and Hamill's Killer, but don't feel despondent if these are not included in your flybox. During the early morning and evening rise, a snip from the necktie which is holding up your trousers or that purple flower on Mother's sun-hat will do the job equally as well. Just get something into the water any way you can, move it a bit, bite a fingernail in anticipation and you're in action. The morning feed normally lasts a couple of hours and it is possible after that first mad flurry that the fishing will show a return to normality for a while. Now is the time to indulge in the picnic hamper, grab forty winks if you feel the urge or take the boat ashore for the comfort stop you've been longing for since dawn but haven't been able to find time for.

From about mid-November, when summer is already beginning to make her presence felt, through until early April, Rotoaira is blessed with a hatch of an insect called the "atonata". Most people refer to them as Darning Needles. About eleven in the morning in November, and earlier as the months become hotter, these orange-and-green inch-or-more-long nymphs—the male is the green fellow—rise from the lake weed to the surface, hesitate while the sun dries their outstretched wings, and then become airborne to settle on the first solid aid to landing they can find. Often it is the boat, and the tiny creatures will practically cover it while they go about the serious business of finding a mate and reproducing. At the moment you see the first few of these on the surface or in the air, the time has come to take up your rod and once again get busy. The trout, I am sure, regard them in the same light as I regard fresh Bluff oysters, and that, I might mention, is with a far from jaundiced eye. Now, you will notice, the trout are swirling, taking those delicacies just under the surface, unhurriedly, deliberately. Don't allow your line to sink too deeply. Make your cast and immediately begin the retrieve. By the time you have gathered a couple of yards, you should be in business.

Lester Colby from Montana, whom you've met elsewhere in this tale, evinced much interest in this type of fishing when we were discussing it during his visit. Ultimately we decided to give it a try on the following day, providing the weather proved suitable for a hatch. By breakfast there was the promise of a warm, relatively windless day and by 10 am we had launched and taken up station behind the island. By 11, the first few signs of a hatch became apparent and

Lester reached for his rod. Now I should mention that where Rotoaira is concerned I am far from being a record-holder. I catch my fair share of fish to be sure, but there must be dozens, perhaps hundreds of anglers who can boast of fish far in excess of my personal best of 7¾ lb. On Taupo and in the surrounding rivers I seem to get my share of the oldtimers and the gourmands, but Rotoaira has always denied me any claim to fame. Each year a select few seem to come up with a fish between 8 lb and double figures, but another season has gone by and my best this year was a paltry 6½.

Lester made his cast in his deceptively casual way, the nymph, which he had tied himself and looked more like an atonata than an atonata, landed like thistledown within inches of a weed patch, settled, and was suddenly borne south-west or thereabout at a steady 20 miles an hour. Les started a tuneless whistle which is a habit of his when he is especially content. He tightened up as much as he could to arrest the flight, but fishing as he was with a 4 x tippet, there was not much chance of giving it the butt.

"Feels like a good one," he said and, knowing his experience with trout, I didn't doubt him. The fish suddenly changed direction to north-east and with Lester retrieving line at a giddy pace, reared out of the water for the first and only time. I was too intent upon my friend's frantically reeling hand to witness anything other than a tail disappearing beneath the surface, but what a tail!

"Thought you said they didn't grow to any great size in Rotoaira?" Les asked, and his eyebrows were where his hairline used to begin.

"No trout in Rotoaira has a tail that big," I told him. "It's obviously malformed."

"For a malformed fish there's a lot of distance between the tail and the head," he retorted, and was then kept at full pressure trying to convince the determined thing that to enter a 10-foot weed clump on one side and exit on the other was not playing the game. Slowly, he was winning, and more and more line was being retrieved on to the reel. The leader was now clear of the water and I stood, net in hand trying to locate the fish. Les brought the rod tip up higher still and there it was, just under the surface, still trying to burrow back to the depths. I nearly fell in. He couldn't do this to me. I'd fished Rotoaira for years and never landed anything to approach this. In the glimpse I'd had, its eyes looked as wide apart as those of a month-old calf. Up it came again, on its side this time, and fearful of the consequences if I fouled up the job of netting it, I waited until it lay almost motionless

"You've got to be joking!" A couple of youngsters display their catch to an oldtimer. Whakapapanui Stream.

The fish we should all love to boast about: a 7-pounder dwarfs the rod and reel.

on the surface. One professional swoop, or so I hoped it looked, and it was ours.

"Nice fish," said Lester, retrieving his nymph from the massive jaw.

"Nice fish?" I bleated. "Nice fish? Is that all you can say? Do you know what you've done? You've done in one confounded cast what I've been trying to do for years! That 'nice fish' as you call it is a couple of pounds heavier than anything I've ever landed on this lake!"

Les looked down at me and a slow grin spread over his face! "Well," he said, "you know the old story about skill beating luck any day. Let this be a lesson to you. But," he added, "if you think its something special, perhaps we'd better take a couple of photographs of it."

I have a colour print of him perching precariously on the stern of my little red boat and holding his fish, a fish which, incidentally, weighed $10\frac{1}{4}$ lbs seven hours after landing, for we had forgotten to take along our scales. For all my professed jealousy, I must say that it couldn't have happened to a nicer fellow. He's welcome back at any time.

During the quieter part of the day, I find that it often pays to shop around, moving the boat 100 yards or so, anchoring, having twenty casts more or less and again changing position. Probably I'm working on the theory that in any school there is a dunce, but it does seem to pay dividends.

The Poutu River is the natural outlet to Rotoaira and with the wind in the other quarter, the small bays on the north side of the stream offer good sport. I have cause to remember an evening up there many years ago. Jo was at that time not as competent with a fly rod as she is now, and we had fished the outlet without much profit before moving around the beach a few hundred yards. My eagle-eyed spouse saw a fish roll only 20 yards from shore, waded out a few feet, made one of her less memorable casts and promptly hooked it. I offered all the advice I could, but as far as I was able to determine, I was either misunderstood or completely ignored. In the event, she landed it safely, if, I thought, rather boastfully, and proceeded to go through the contortions she thought necessary to project a line.

I, meantime, had with what I hoped appeared nonchalant ease, cast halfway to the far end of the lake and was retrieving with supreme confidence in the result. Jo let out a nervous squeak, something exploded out of the water not 5 feet in front of me, and away out there my fly fetched up firmly embedded in an old Maori canoe or something equally immovable.

This was getting embarrassing. Mumbling to myself, I tied on another lure, making certain that it matched Jo's in every respect, and made another cast. My wife obviously did not realise just how shattering those two fish had been to my ego, nor that I had decided that her weekly allowance was altogether too extravagant. I watched in condescending superiority as she bumbled out her interpretation of a cast, saw the fly hit the water like a rock avalanche and felt my own fly drag into a weedbed. Retrieving quickly to remove the pesky stuff, I glanced over my shoulder. "O *no*," I thought, but there was no disputing the fact Jo's rod was bent in the arc that only a fish can impart. That married woman with whom I lived, I decided, was in danger of walking home, if, indeed she still had a home to go to.

I have been comprehensively outfished in my day, but never quite as blatantly and shamelessly as I was during those couple of hours on Rotoaira. Jo had seven before I came out of my daze and reasoned that I was overcasting the fish. They were in close, probably only 20 feet from our boots and she was tossing that fly right down their greedy mouths. She took her tenth and limit fish, returned it to the water, I beached my third and we headed for home. A few miles down the road she started to giggle. "There's no justice, is there?" she asked. "You were casting beautifully and getting nothing and I was doing everything wrong and getting fish." Oh, the scheming, cunning wench knew how many beans made five. She'd have to live with me for a few years yet and knew that flattery would get her somewhere.

"If I promise to really work on my casting so that you will be proud of me, will you take me fishing again?" she cooed.

"You bet I'll take you fishing again, girl," I thought, "if only to prove to you that skill is an integral part of catching trout."

"I bought some nice steak today and some mushrooms," she burbled on. "I'll cook a fillet mignon when we get home and follow it up with apple pie and that thick farm cream."

Well, a fellow wouldn't get far in front of a divorce judge by petitioning that his wife hooked more fish than he did. Imagine it.

"Who brings this petition?"

"I do, your honour."

"What is the nature of your complaint?"

"Mental cruelty."

Fred Goddard, angler supreme from the State of Washington, USA, with his 13½-pound, 29½-inch three-year-old fish from the Tarawera River, Lake Tarawera and . . . *Below:* . . . another view of the most perfectly proportioned trout the author has ever seen.

"Elucidate, if you please."

"Well, your honour, Jo—that's my wife, or the one I'm here to discard—and I went trout fishing. She landed seven before I got even the semblance of a strike. Further she showed neither remorse nor shame. She has boasted of it to relatives, friends, acquaintances and complete strangers, thus placing me in a position where I am the object of ridicule and snide remarks. No longer can I be regarded as any sort of authority on the piscatorial arts."

"Hmm, I see your point. I have the same problem when my wife challenges me to the hammer throw. However, I feel I must question the defendant. Now, Mrs Jensen, do you dispute the facts as they were presented?"

"No, your honour, but I should state in mitigation that I am basking in this new-found glory because for years I have had to listen to my husband proclaiming to all and sundry how I couldn't beat him at golf, even if he handicapped himself by playing one-handed with a hockey stick."

"Well, well, well. This puts a totally different complexion on things. And have you witnesses to this heinous conduct?"

"Every man, woman and child in Turangi, your honour."

"I see. It appears to me that the wrong person is petitioning and that Mrs Jensen has grounds for a counter-claim. Mrs Jensen, do you still wish to share the same roof with this villain?"

"Providing he does his bragging only in whispers and in the bath with the taps running, your honour."

"I doubt the wisdom of your decision, my dear, but it is indeed a brave one. I find for the defendant. Costs will be against the petitioner in the form of three smoked trout and a reduction of two strokes in handicap. Next case."

If only I had known that the Judge's wife gave him two strokes a hole and invariably beat him by the time they reached the twelfth!

I've never given Jo the sort of shellacking she dealt out to me that day at Rotoaira, but occasionally when she is feeling tender towards me she holds back and lets me finish the day a fish or two in front. At least, that's what she tells me, anyway.

Like anywhere else, fish are where you find them and this holds good at Rotoaira too. They are inclined to school perhaps more than elsewhere, but if you keep to the windward shore and experiment at different depths and varying speeds of retrieve you will find it easier to limit out with a fly rod here than anywhere else I know.

There are times however, when a small spinner seems to attract those Rotoaira trout far better than any fly ever manufactured. With a threadline rod I'm about as effective as Twiggy would be at shot-putting, but many of my clients bring their gear along and want to use it. The Rotoaira season extends from 1 August until 30 June, and August, September and October, together with May and June, seem particularly kind to this method. I learned just how effective it can be when Bob Biddle and I were asked by the Government Tourist Bureau to provide some action shots of fish for a camera crew. That was one film where I'm pretty sure I had a walk-on and walk-off part, or perhaps they managed to eradicate me altogether. Bob had taken along a spinning rod and I was armed with the inevitable fly tackle. Before our arrival Bob had seen fish moving a few hundred yards from the launching ramp and our small armada took up station. I cast downwind, Bob lobbed his spinner towards the boat holding the cameras, and we were away.

Bob caught a fish which jumped to order a few times and ensured happy smiles from the crew. I reeled in and, while smiling encouragement, tried to make sure I had my good side to the lenses. Trouble was, I didn't know whether I had a good side. Bob landed it, held it up while the crew expended film as if they were shooting a sequel to *Gone with the Wind*, and we cast again. Same result. Never mind, I'd get them some red-hot footage when I tangled with one on my new 8-footer. I'd show them how a fish should be played. Bob caught another. I think my casting may have become a little ragged about that time. The way those boys were running film there would be precious little left for me.

Bob, I should mention for the benefit of those who haven't met him, is a Maori. He was also, I was finding out in humiliation, a damned mean exponent of spinning. Race relationships in New Zealand do not leave a lot to be desired but, I decided, this was developing into a situation where the Treaty of Waitangi was seriously in jeopardy. I cast. Bob caught a fish. I cast, Why hadn't I brought that spinning tackle? Bob caught a fish.

"I think we've got as much footage as we need," some fool called from the other boat.

"Calls himself a director," I mumbled under my breath.

"Why don't you borrow Bob's rod and pick one up Tony?" came

the same loathsome voice. Unwillingly I allowed the thing to be passed to me: I'd show them that any fool could catch trout on this equipment. "Damned things should be made illegal anyway." I thought.

My first cast was a dandy—long, effortless, confidently executed. If only the other boat had been in a different position it would undoubtedly have yielded a fish far bigger than any caught previously. There were snorts of alarm as the spinner clattered into the tripod of a camera. They dropped it overboard for me, hurt expressions on their faces. I could see that they thought I was a very poor loser. The next one was not as spectacular, nor did it gain maximum velocity. I nearly lost the sight of my right eye.

For the uneducated, there is a most annoying gadget on a fixed-spool or coffee-grinder-type reel. It's called a bale-arm. Before casting, the idea is to swing this cleverly camouflaged piece of no. eight fencing-wire over to the opposite side, allowing the monofilament to run free behind the parabolic arc of the spinner. Well, I didn't and that lethal piece of hardware performed the tightest parabola ever seen off a drawing board. Shaken to the core, with trembling hands I remedied the oversight, aimed at 180 degrees from the other boat, snapped my wrist into it like an expert and watched it sail majestically on its journey. It landed with the same plop as Bob's had done, not quite as far, certainly, but nevertheless adequately far from its source to hint at a professional presentation. I began the retrieve.

"Cover that equipment," someone yelled. "Come on, before it's all ruined with the rain." I had noticed the odd drop on the rather wide parting in my hair but had been too busy to worry about it. Now it had started in earnest. Another couple of turns of the handle and it happened. A strike, and a good one.

"Got one," I hollered, "I've got a beauty." At my back I heard the motor of the other boat roar into life. They would be manoeuvering to the most advantageous position, I knew, but they were taking a damned long time about it. I risked a glance over my shoulder. A hundred yards away at 30 knots or thereabouts the camera boat was heading for shore and shelter like a homing pigeon for its loft. Bob, moreover, was retrieving our anchor as if his life depended upon it.

"Of all the ungrateful boors," I thought. "Can't even stand a few spots of rain." The fact that my shirt was beginning to feel like a sponge was of no importance.

"The hell with them," I murmured. I'd still bring in the best fish of the day. It rose then and I knew my moment of triumph had arrived. It made the others Bob had caught look like Norwegian sardines. This one I wanted so badly that it hurt. It turned away from the boat and kept going and going and going—and so it should have: free of the spinner there really was nothing to stop it. For all I know it is still going. Bob started the motor and a few minutes later we were all drying out in his office. Everyone seemed happy with the day's fishing. Someone produced a bottle of good cheer. I sulked.

About two hours and another bottle later the director came over to me. "I want to thank you, Tony," he said.

"Oh yes," I thought, "this guy's a real diplomat."

"Yes," he said, "that blue shirt you're wearing really gave us that little bit of colour against the white boat that we needed."

And he wasn't even trying to be funny.

Because the lake is only 55 feet at its deepest part, trollers on Rotoaira get a more satisfying return for their money than their counterparts on Taupo. No necessity here for 100 yards of line trailed behind the boat, indeed I know of only one area where 50 yards of lead line can be used without dredging weed from the bottom. Of a consequence, trollers get a lot more action from the fish. However, nine times out of ten, regular fly tackle harled at fairly slow speeds will take all the trout you can comfortably use. On occasion it will take a while to find a school but, once found, double, and indeed treble strikes are not uncommon.

I recall one visit I made to the lake which left me overcome with embarrassment and brought home to one of the party the realisation that there are clothes designed for Fifth Avenue shopping and others eminently more suitable for a day's fishing in a small boat.

I had launched and was waiting to begin the day when my clients were delivered to the ramp in their chauffeur-driven limousine. Father, Mother and Junior alighted and introductions were completed.

They made a strange family. Dad was nothing short of gay (not in the gay-lib sense of the word), for his overpowering floral shirt, baggy purple shorts and business shoes on bare feet did appear a trifle incongruous and inappropriate on a dull, cool morning. He was already shivering slightly. Junior was practically invisible facially. A dense mass of fungus completely hid him from view and hair a couple of feet long completed the camouflage. One large gold earring protruded through the jungle, presumably attached to something. He wore his Sunday best of a sleeveless sweater, jeans ripped off below the knees and multicoloured tattoos. Mom was something else again. The first thing I noticed were the diamonds. She did not have one in her left nostril, but every finger sported a few and the bundle of enormous stones which constituted her earrings were sufficiently heavy to stretch the lobes to two inches. Her attire was straight Schiaparelli. A canary-yellow top cut by a master led down to dazzlingly white culottes which in turn surmounted white shoes with a platform sole not less than 4 inches high.

Dad marched, Junior padded, and Mom teetered down to the boat and we headed for the far shore. It was about noon when the adults had a double strike. Amidst all the consternation and excitement, both fish were flapping madly alongside the boat as I attempted to net the first. I made a successful lunge, gilled the fish the more easily to remove the lure, turned quickly to net the other and somehow or other managed to throw the first towards the fish tin. It wasn't until I stood triumphant with the second in the net that I realised what an indifferent shot I had made: Mom was gazing down horrified at her ensemble and a still flapping, copiously bleeding trout was embedded somewhere between her generous thighs. There are days when it is preferable to hit the alarm on the head and stay in bed all day.

Fishing is expensive by New Zealand standards on Rotoaira. Two dollars a day per rod or 25 dollars for a full 10-month season doesn't stand up alongside the 75 cents a day and 7 dollars for year-round fishing anywhere in the Taupo basin, but there is one thing certain: you'll catch a lot of fish and you'll have a lot of fun doing it.

CHAPTER 15

KNOTS

IT IS IMPOSSIBLE to emphasise too strongly the importance of the correct knots for fly fishing. There are three basic ones, all of which are easy to tie after a little practice and all of which provide the two ingredients we require most; strength and a disinclination to slip.

When tying the fly to the leader tippet, the clinch knot is the most widely used, although the turtle knot is probably the stronger. Illustrations of both are given and it's over to you to make your choice. Remember though, that if you decide upon the clinch, at least 6 and preferably more turns of the leader around itself should be used. Fewer than 6 and once in a while you will find that a trout has departed with the fly and you are left only with a feeling of frustration.

CLINCH KNOT

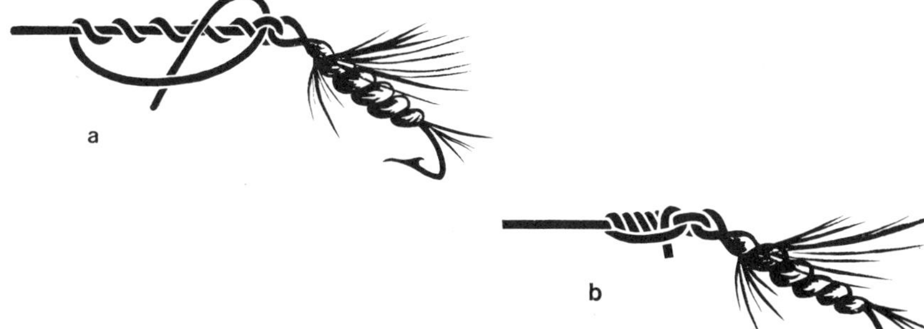

A simple fast and effective knot for tying the fly to the leader.

(a) Pass the end of the leader through the eye of the hook and make at least six turns before passing the end through the original loop.
(b) Pull up until snug against the eye and snip off any surplus. Quickly undone by using nails of thumb and index finger and pulling in direction of line and leader.

TURTLE KNOT

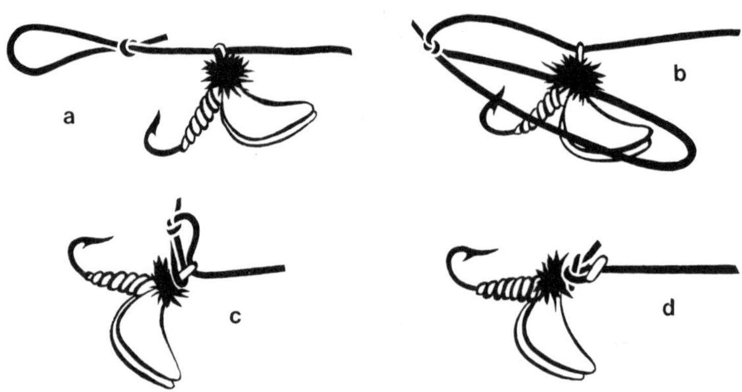

Preferred by many as a stronger knot than the clinch for tying fly to leader.

(a) Pass tippet of leader through eye of fly and fashion a single running knot in end.
(b) Pass the fly through the loop formed and
(c) Pull up loop until it is resting on the neck of the hook.
(d) Making sure that the loop remains against the neck, pull tight and snip off end of loop.

The blood knot is used for tying sections of leader together. The majority of New Zealanders rarely use a tapered leader, preferring the simplicity of pulling off the required number of feet from a spool of monofilament and making do with that. What they do not realise, of course, is that the tapered one will roll over correctly as the cast is made, thus ensuring a far better presentation of the fly. I do encourage those of you who don't use the blood knot to start doing so. It's simple, quick and strong, and if you do tangle with a snag, only the tippet needs to be retied instead of the whole leader, as is so often the case. Once again, at least 6 turns on each side is recommended and don't forget to test each knot after it is tied.

The nail knot is not used extensively by our fishermen either, and yet it is one which should be. It is the ideal for tying the leader to the fly line or the fly line to the backing. Our anglers, almost without exception, use a loop in the end of the leader through which they make a figure-of-eight knot with the end of the fly line. The disadvantages are many. The knot created by the fly line is bulky and can not be wound through the small tip ring of the rod. The figure-of eight is sometimes pulled so tight that it becomes impossible to

BLOOD KNOT

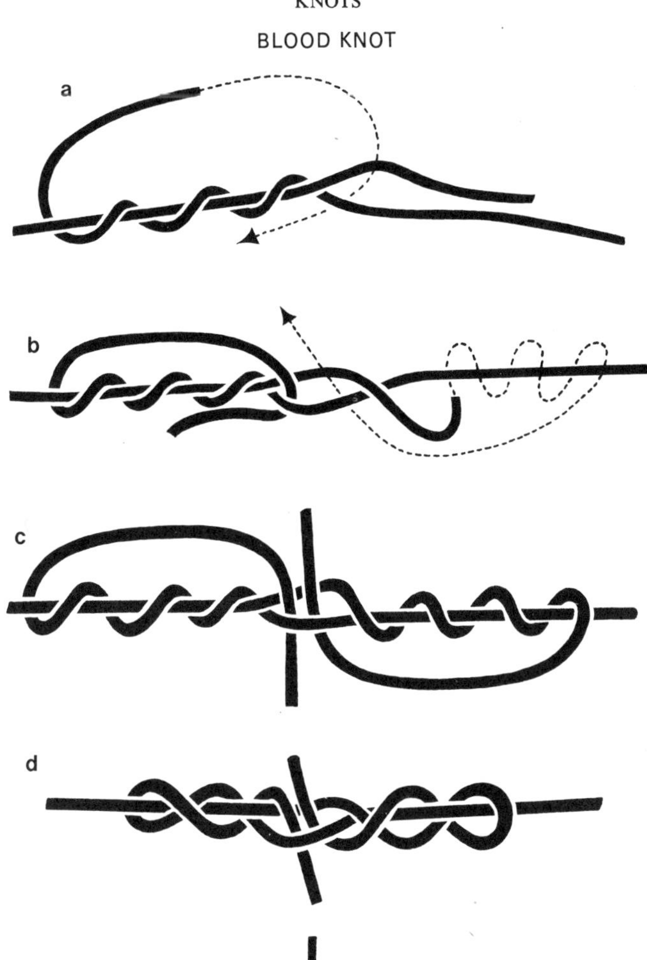

This is the knot employed when two or more sections of leader are to be joined.

(a) Overlap the two sections and wrap one around the other at least six times (only three wraps are shown in the diagram). Take the end through the gap at the crossover and hold firmly between thumb and finger.
(b & c) Now, making the reverse wraps with the other piece of leader take the end once again through the same loop as (a).
(d) Gently pull both ends simultaneously and make the knot snug.
(e) Test the knot by a steady pull from both ends and then each end separately. Snip off excess.

untie and is clipped off, thus progressively shortening the taper of an expensive fly line. Worse still, the knot in the loop of the leader becomes the weakest point if a level leader is being employed and, nine times out of ten, this is where the break will occur.

So let's become modern Boy Scouts and learn to use the nail knot. It doesn't slip if tied securely, it will run through the guides comfortably and smoothly, and if you use fairly heavy nylon in the first section of the leader, it probably won't have to be changed more than a couple of times a season.

NAIL KNOT

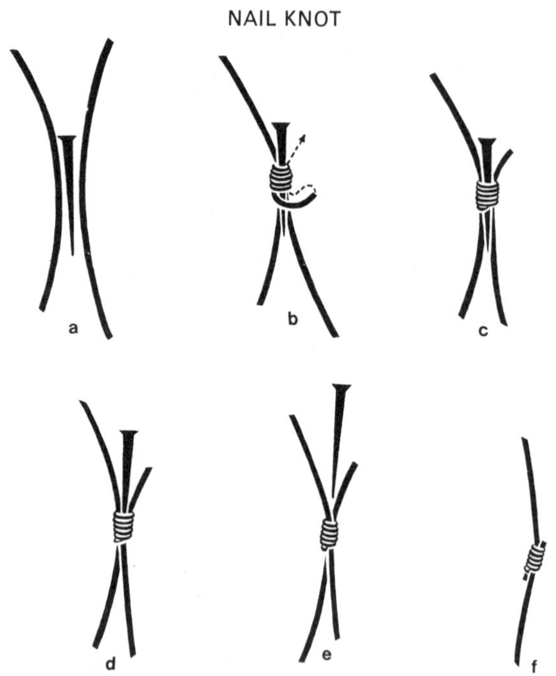

The finest knot for attaching the leader to the fly line.

(a) Using a tapered nail place line and leader parallel to nail.
(b) Winding downward wrap leader around line, nail and itself at least six times and tuck end of leader up under coils (dotted line).
(c) Pull firmly on both ends of the leader and snug knot down on to the nail.
(d) Slowly commence extraction of nail at the same time firming up knot by pulling on both ends of the leader.
(e) Remove nail and again tighten knot.
(f) Snip off ends of line and leader.

There are not too many areas in New Zealand where a dropper is legal, but I have been asked so often to explain the knot for attaching one that I feel it should be illustrated here. It is easy to tie and when pulled up snug against the body knot of the main leader shows no tendency to move.

DROPPER KNOT

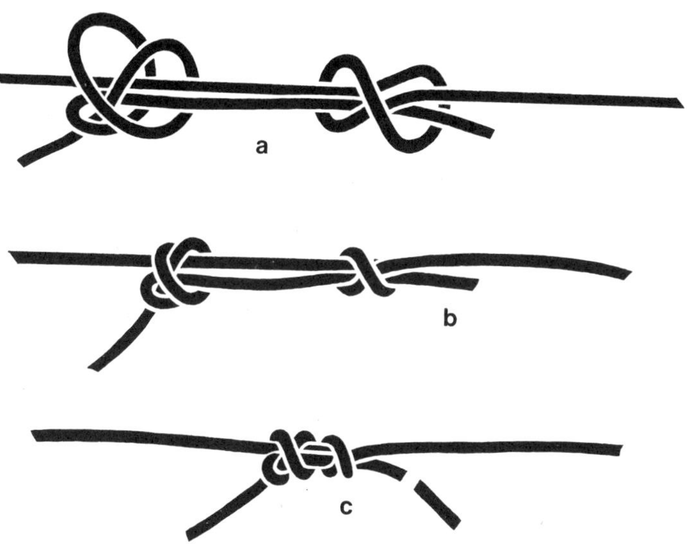

This is the knot used when an additional leader is required for wet fly or nymph fishing.

(a) Make two loops of the dropper around the leader and take the end through the figure eight of the main leader.
(b) Pull up on short end of dropper to tighten and draw both knots together until snug.
(c) Pull on dropper only to test firmness and cut off short end.

For my money the knots described here are the best available for the job they set out to do, and the clinch (or the Turtle), the blood and the nail should become as natural and as essential to you as cleaning your teeth.

Let me repeat though: test each knot thoroughly before you make that first cast.

CHAPTER 16

THE CONDITION FACTOR CHART

NEW ZEALANDERS, when discussing a fish they have caught, invariably describe it as being so-and-so pounds and ounces. In many parts of the USA, they worry not a jot about the weight, but tell you of a beauty of "x" number of inches.

Personally, I like to assess a fish by its condition, i.e. the weight of a fish against its length. In other words, a fish of 5 lb in weight which is only 21 inches long has thrived and is in superb condition. A fish of the same weight which measures 25 inches is a thoroughly poor specimen and should either be returned to the water in the hope that it will recover or removed and buried in the back garden. The former will have firm, salmon-coloured flesh and will be a gourmet's joy, the latter will make a hungry tomcat turn away in disdain.

Basically then the Condition Chart is a guide to inform you whether your fish is outstanding, average or poor. Generalising, it states that a fish above 60 on the scale is one that you can boast of for many a year to come, between 50 and 60 is a fish in excellent condition, one of between 40 and 50 is run-of-the-mill and anything under 40 is a throw-back. The chart is based upon the following equation which looks complicated but projects figures we can all understand:

$$\text{CONDITION FACTOR} = \frac{\text{WEIGHT (POUNDS)} \times 100{,}000}{\text{LENGTH}^3 \text{ (INCHES)}} \quad \Big| \quad \frac{\text{WEIGHT (GRAMS)} \times 3612.8}{\text{LENGTH}^3 \text{ (CENTIMETRES)}}$$

If you should be in the habit of recording a diary of your fishing exploits, a season-by-season assessment can be made of the quality of the trout in your particular area. Are they improving? Are they declining? The condition factor chart will give you the answer more readily than your memory can possibly do. Why not use it?

TROUT CONDITION FACTORS GENERAL TABLES

WEIGHT IN GRAMS

Length in centimetres	450	675	900	1125	1350	1575	1800	2025	2250	2475	2700	2925	3150	3375	3600	3825	4050	4275	4500	4725	4950	5175	5400	5625	5850	6075	6300	6525	6750	Length in inches (approx.)
30	60	90																												12
31	54	81																												
32	49	74	99																											
33	45	67	90																											13
34	41	62	82																											
35	37	56	75	94																										
36	34	52	69	87																										
37	32	48	64	80	96																									
38	29	44	59	74	88																									15
39	27	41	54	68	82	95																								
40	25	38	50	63	76	88																								
41	23	35	47	58	70	82	94																							
42	21	32	43	54	65	76	87	98																						
43	20	30	40	51	61	71	81	92																						17
44		28	38	47	57	66	76	85	95																					
45		26	35	44	53	62	71	80	89	98																				
46		25	33	41	50	58	66	75	83	91																				
47		23	31	39	46	54	62	70	78	86	93																			
48		22	29	36	44	51	58	66	73	80	88																			19
49		20	27	34	41	48	55	62	69	76	82	89	96																	
50			26	32	39	45	52	58	65	71	78	84	91																	
51			24	30	36	42	49	55	61	67	73	79	85	91																20
52			23	28	34	40	46	52	57	63	69	75	80	86																
53			21	27	32	38	43	49	54	60	65	70	76	81	87	92														
54			20	25	30	36	41	46	51	56	61	67	72	77	82	87														
55				24	29	34	39	43	48	53	58	63	68	73	78	83	87	92												
56				23	27	32	37	41	46	50	55	60	64	69	74	78	83	87	92	97										22
57				21	26	30	35	39	43	48	52	57	61	65	70	74	79	83	87	92										
58				20	24	29	33	37	41	45	49	54	58	62	66	70	74	79	83	87	91	95								
59					23	27	31	35	39	43	47	51	55	59	63	67	71	75	79	83	87	91								
60					22	26	30	33	37	41	45	48	52	56	60	63	67	71	75	79	82	86	90							
61					21	25	28	32	35	39	42	46	50	53	57	60	64	68	71	75	78	82	85							24
62					20	23	27	30	34	37	40	44	47	51	54	57	61	64	68	71	75	78	81	85	89					
63						22	26	29	32	35	39	42	45	48	52	55	58	61	65	68	71	74	78	81	85	88				
64						21	24	27	31	34	37	40	43	46	49	52	55	58	62	65	68	71	74	77	80	83	86	89		
65						20	23	26	29	32	35	38	41	44	47	50	53	56	59	62	65	68	71	73	76	79	82	85		
66							22	25	28	31	33	36	39	42	45	48	50	53	56	59	62	65	67	70	73	76	79	81	84	26
	1		2		3		4		5		6		7		8		9		10		11		12		13		14		15	

WEIGHT IN POUNDS (APPROX.) : ½ POUND INTERVALS

By courtesy of the Wildlife Service, NZ Dept. of Internal Affairs.

CHAPTER 17

REMINDERS AND RECOMMENDATIONS

THIS IS NOT INTENDED to be a precis of all that has gone before, but if it serves as a cross-reference, so much the better.

Do:

Purchase tackle which will give you pleasure to use throughout many seasons. It is rarely that lower-priced equipment is satisfactory or durable. Having made the selection, maintain it in good order.

Practise those essential basic casts until they become second nature in any situation in which you may find yourself.

Observe fishing etiquette at all times. Become known as a river hog or a boor and the reputation will stick to you for many a season.

Sacrifice a few minutes of your own precious fishing time to help the young and the inexperienced. They will appreciate a word or two of advice and we can all recall our own clumsy attempts at the beginning of our angling careers.

Study the water to be fished before moving in, and try and estimate where fish should be lying. Remember they like a deep, quiet spot where they need a minimum of effort to maintain position.

Fish all the water by starting with a few short casts to trout which could be lying in close to your bank.

Make sure that the river bottom is clearly visible when wading a pool which you do not know intimately. Waders are not designed as an aid to swimming.

Utilise a wading-stick of some sort if crossing heavy water. That third leg has saved many cold and miserable dunkings and a few possible fatalities.

Keep downstream of the pool when trying to ascertain if there are fish lying in the smaller streams.

Study the technique being used by other anglers if they are hooking fish and you are not. Ask yourself if they are casting more upstream or down than you are. Try and sneak a look at their flies or the length of their leaders and compare with your own.

Use a longer leader than normal when fishing in low clear water. Use a shorter one than you would habitually do when the river is running high or is discoloured.

Make sure you use the knots suggested and ascertain they are snug and unlikely to slip before you commence fishing.

Limit your kill to the fish you can comfortably eat.

Keep your hands free of the gills if you intend to return the fish to the water.

Kill the older fish in preference to the maidens.

Read your fishing licence and make sure you understand the precis of the Taupo Fishing Regulations thereon. Better still, obtain a copy of the Regulations themselves.

Buy a copy of the booklet *Safety in Small Craft* if you are a boat-owner, and adhere to the suggestions and requirements it puts forward.

Maintain respect for both river and lake at all times.

Dress sensibly and warmly for the conditions. It's far easier to disrobe if too hot, than to wish you had brought along some warm clothing.

Remain well back from the lip if wading at the Delta or any stream mouth.

Let the fish come close to you during smelting rather than drive them ahead of you into deep water.

If trolling, buy and use that reference map. You'll catch more fish if you do.

Practise an anti-litter policy around our waterways yourself and frown on others who despoil them with beer cans, bottles, paper and plastic bags.

Undertake by every means in your power to fight long and hard to preserve, maintain and improve the angling in the area and to oppose any group or faction which threatens it.

Final Note

Much has been left unsaid which might have been said. Possibly much has been stressed far beyond the point of boredom. For these sins of omission and commission I apologise, and trust that they have not been too numerous. All that now remains is to hope that someone somewhere has gleaned a little angling knowledge from the preceding pages, and to wish you all "Tight Lines on the Tongariro"!

OTHER REED BOOKS FOR FISHERMEN

TAUPO FISHING GUIDE by James Siers and John Sierpinski. A modestly-priced but comprehensive guide to the lake and its tributary rivers. Liberally illustrated.

TROUT FLIES IN NEW ZEALAND by Keith Draper. A guide to all the artificial lures, wet and dry flies and nymphs used in this country, with a most useful chapter on entomology. Many drawings, four pages of colour plates.

THE ANGLER'S COOKBOOK: TROUT, SALMON AND EEL by Stewart Reidpath. By an angler for anglers who may cook the catch on a riverbank campfire, or on the back-garden barbecue, or on the kitchen stove for serving on a festive dinnertable.

A GUIDE TO MODELMAKING AND TAXIDERMY by Leo Cappel. Fascinating to the angler/handyman—skin and stuff your catch, or cast it in rubber.

SEA ANGLER'S GUIDE by Ray Doogue and John Moreland. Full information on tackle and techniques, with detailed descriptions of over one hundred sport and food fish, and many line drawings.

HOOK LINE AND SINKER by Ray Doogue—the great all-embracing guide to seafishing in New Zealand coastal waters. Generously illustrated with photographs, drawings, charts and diagrams.

SEA FISHING FOR BEGINNERS by Ray Doogue. In this case the fishing is for saltwater tyros. Packed with essential information, modestly priced.

THE SCREAM OF THE REEL, compiled by Jack Pollard. The great anthology of fishing stories of New Zealand and Australia—truth and fiction, prose and poetry, salt and freshwater, big-game fish and tiddlers, classic cartoons, sketches and photos.

LEGEND OF TONGARIRO RIVER MAP
Drawing only—not to scale :—
1. Fence Pool
2. Whitikau Pool
3. Sand Pool
4. Blue Pool
5. Fan Pool
6. Cliff Pool
7. Poutu Pool
8. Red Hut Pool
9. Shag Pool
10. Duchess Pool
11. Silly Pool
12. Upper Birch Pool
13. Lower Birch Pool
14. Cattle Rustlers Pool
15. Stag Pool
16. Admirals Pool
17. Kamahi Pool
18. The Boulevard
19. Hydro Pool
20. Breakfast Pool
21. Major Jones Pool
22. Island Pool
23. Lonely Pool
24. Groin Pool
25. Bridge Pool
26. Swirl Pool
27. The Stones
28. Log Pool
29. Reed Pool
30. Jones Pool
31. The "Lake"
32. de Latour's Pool
33. de Latour's Reach
34. Down's Pool
35. Grace's Pool
36. The Bend
37. Poplar Pool
38. Cherry Pool
39. Dan's Pool
40 (a) Delta: Main Mouth
40 (b) Delta: The Hook
40 (c) Delta: First Mouth
40 (d) Delta: Blind Mouth
A
B
C
D
E
F
G
H
I
J